THE ART OF KITCHEN DESIGN

Is the kitchen a work space or a living space? Most people today would surely answer that it's both – the average household spends more time in the kitchen than any other room in the home. Yet in many houses and apartments the kitchen is the Cinderella room – at best a purely functional area to be clothed in efficient-looking 'fitted' cupboards, units and surfaces – or cluttered with unattractive tables and stools.

In *The Art of Kitchen Design*, leading kitchen architect Johnny Grey sounds a rousing note of liberation for the kitchen and shows, fascinatingly, that a kitchen can be efficient and contemporary yet at the same time offer traditional comforts and style as an elegant living space.

Johnny Grey finds his inspiration from many sources, including the traditional country kitchens of rural Scandinavia, the American Arts and Crafts Movement and the farm-house kitchens of Britain which evolved naturally as family rooms providing warmth, comfort and company as well as hearty meals for healthy country appetites. In his approach to kitchen design, he demonstrates that timeless freestanding dressers and cupboards can do as good or better a job than lookalike commercial kits, while being more responsive to the individual space concerned.

Lavishly illustrated throughout with over 150 superb colour photographs, the book shows 'unfitted' kitchen solutions working in every type of kitchen space – from large and lofty to small and awkward. As well as presenting case studies, it is full of intriguing new ideas that will interest not only anyone planning a new kitchen but also designers, architects, decorators and craft enthusiasts. Beautifully designed and produced, *The Art of Kitchen Design* combines tradition and contemporary designs in ways that will help every reader make their kitchen a joy to be in.

Johnny Grey is the leading designer and producer of kitchens in the UK. He trained as an architect and has wide-ranging design interests, with a particular enthusiasm for kitchens – a strong early influence was his aunt, the food writer Elizabeth David. In the mid-1980s he worked closely with the influential kitchen designers Smallbone of Devizes, and has since received major honours in the USA and Great Britain, including an award from New York's *Metropolitan Home* magazine as 'the world's best kitchen designer'. He now lives in Sussex with his wife and three children, and runs a design practice specializing in state-of-the-art kitchens and interior architecture.

Jacket photography by Peter Aprahamian

THE ART OF KITCHEN DESIGN

Johnny Grey

WARD LOCK

To my late parents and my immediate family
for their love and support, in particular
Becca, my wife, and also for the healing skills
of the late Dr Raja Srivastava who helped me
through a difficult illness. This book is also
for all the wonderful clients who have given
me the chance to work in their homes and for
all the craftspeople who turned the design
into reality.

This revised and updated edition first published in the
UK 1999 by Ward Lock

First edition 1994
Reprinted (with revisions) 1995 (twice)
First paperback edition 1995

Text copyright © 1994, 1995, 1999
Design and layout © Ward Lock 1994, 1995, 1999

The picture acknowledgements on page 206
constitute an extension to this copyright page

Distributed in the United States by
Sterling Publishing Co., Inc.
387 Park Avenue South, New York, NY 10016-8810

A CIP catalogue record for this book is available from
the British Library

ISBN 0 7063 7839 3 (hbk)

Designed by James Campus

Printed and bound in DELO Tiskarna by arrangement
with Korotan Ljubljana

Ward Lock Illustrated Division
The Orion Publishing Group
Wellington House
125 Strand
London WC2R 0BB

Contents

Introduction

In this revised and expanded edition, I have attempted to bring together many of the strands that are part of the kitchen design process: historical and social traditions, cooking habits, design ergonomics, architectural sensibilities and the broader cultural contribution that goes towards making up our idea of a comfortable home life. *The Art of Kitchen Design* is not a 'how to' book. It is a profile of the kitchen as a room that is alternately down-to-earth and reaches for the sky. This new, expanded edition is tipped a little more towards the practical; of three new sections, the longest is devoted to planning so that everyone can move towards creating their own dream kitchen, whether alone or with the help of a designer.

My first contribution to the public debate on the nature of kitchen design took the form of the concept of the unfitted kitchen, an idea I launched in 1987. It was seen by many as a turning point in the perception of the role of the kitchen as more than a food laboratory, and in recognition of the fact that this room was becoming a social space as well.

If one's life is busy and centred around a happy household where is the time for separate activities with dedicated rooms for each? The new kitchen is now a multi-purpose space, a living room by another name and it is at the heart of the home today because of its social functions. The need for private rooms is important in a home and the failure to recognize this fact contributed to the demise of the idea of the open plan house. But some rooms are public spaces for community living and the kitchen has a unique role in combining two social functions: living, in the broadest sense, and eating. Ironically, it may be bringing us back towards a different kind of open-planned house, where the designation of the function of space is freer.

Throughout history, rooms have evolved, changed names and altered in size and location. Aspects of their purpose have migrated from one space to another; this applies to the kitchen today. Every time I visit a new client I find that their interpretation of what a kitchen is for them is unique. It is a response to their house layout, the stage they are at with their lives, their climate and their cultural traditions. The kitchen is a tremendously flexible concept, although the word itself is inconveniently fixed, perhaps we need a new word for what the kitchen is today. For my late aunt, Elizabeth David, it was called a study kitchen, for some it is really a living room, in the broadest sense, with a food preparation section attached.

I find the sociology of home life fascinating but I am also intrigued as to how it all might change. In my book *The Hardworking House*, I have expanded my investigation into the other rooms in the house. In response to many people I have met, particularly at recent public talks I have given in the US, I have included a new section on the kitchen of the future. In my opinion, a comfortable kitchen is one of the necessities of a civilized life and a major contributor to a happy household. It is after all a refuge, a creative space, a cradle of sociability and hospitality, a place synonymous with sustenance and a room that offers a constancy against the backdrop of the ebb and flow of family life.

I have had great pleasure in learning about design from many teachers. During my six years of study at the Architectural Association School of Architecture in London I gained much from my tutors Jeremy Dixon, Chris Cross, Mike Gold and Tony Dugdale. I must also pay a handsome tribute to my late aunt, Elizabeth David OBE, whose erudite intelligence inspired me in so many ways. Many of my clients have generously given me not only the opportunity to carry out sometimes rather experimental ideas, but the chance to share their own inspired vision. Over the years, those I have worked with have contributed many useful ideas, particularly the furniture maker Jonathan Morriss and all the members of my design team, including Will Jameson, David Richards, Mike Rooke, Ethan Maynard, the artist Lucy Turner, and my trustworthy administrator Anna Moore. My wife Becca who comes from a respected Australian architectural family has helped me focus on design issues that really matter.

I suspect that we lost our way a little in the 1960s and 1970s. I hope that this book will help in a small way, to get us back onto the right path again. I hope too, that it provides you with inspiration and stimulation, and makes a contribution to your understanding of the rich tradition of the kitchen.

Johnny Grey

Rogate, Petersfield, Hants, UK
San Francisco Design Centre, USA
www.johnnygreykitchens.com

I

SOCIABLE ROLE OF THE KITCHEN

THE origins of the kitchen lie in the hearth. The miracle of fire brought us not only the flame for cooking, but also warmth for survival in winter. From the early hunter-gatherer societies and the subsequent development of agriculture the preparation, cooking and eating of food have provided punctuation for the day; coming together to eat is an expression of man's natural gregariousness. The obvious pleasure in eating is heightened by making oneself comfortable while doing so. By involving others the enjoyment is extended further, for eating by oneself is a lonely act. This is why the immediate physical environment surrounding the eating and cooking of food is so important, and part of the expression of a deep-rooted tradition.

The word kitchen is inadequate but we are stuck with it for the time being at least. In coining a phrase such as the sociable or unfitted kitchen I was hoping to open up the concept of the kitchen as a room. This does not just mean the absence of continuously fitted cupboards hastily bolted on to the perimeter walls. There is a substantial philosophy behind the concept: it is the search for a sound set of ideas or values. This is important because so much has gone wrong with kitchen design in the last thirty years. Brutal, uncomfortable and inhuman kitchens have been sold relentlessly on the back of clever marketing and hungry production lines. How can yards of melamine ruthlessly repeated in the same geometric configuration and colour produce a place comfortable enough to embrace the wider meaning of this word 'kitchen' and fulfil the many uses we expect from a contemporary kitchen?

Apart from talking, sitting, eating and cooking, there are myriad other activities such as children doing their homework or playing with toys, making telephone calls, ironing, dealing with household correspondence, bottling or preserving jams or condiments, entertaining friends or simply spending a few minutes catching up with your newspaper or book. I even distinctly recall seeing my mother dozing off on quite a few occasions at the end of a long day, and certainly no kitchen is truly complete without at least one comfortable chair, or wherever possible a sofa!

In 1976 an eccentric friend of mine, the grandson of a famous poet, asked me to make him a kitchen to suit a well-preserved Edwardian house, which he had just bought in Tooting, London. It had all its original features: stained glass, tiles, mouldings, raised plaster ceilings, textured wallpaper. It had been in the hands of one owner since it was built. The kitchen to suit my friend's personality and house could hardly be a laminated plastic fitted 'dream kitchen' which was all that was available commercially at the time. It was my first kitchen, albeit Gothic and rather hurriedly put together. It consisted of two rooms linked together; the cooking part and the eating/food storage area. The key problem was the shortage of space, but through the use of free-standing furniture in the

eating area I learned that an illusion of spaciousness could be achieved by leaving space around each piece of furniture, rather than fitting cupboards from wall to wall.

I learned too that a mixture of free-standing items of furniture with a judicious use of built-in pieces (the room had a width of 9 ft/2.75 metres in the cooking area) could result in a practical design but with relaxing features too such as a rack hanging from the ceiling and shelves rather than eye-level cupboards on the wall. So in brief, my much publicized concept of the unfitted kitchen was born. A well-planned mixture of free-standing furniture and architectural fittings form its philosophical basis. There has been much development and refinement since then, but in planning terms these relate back to what I discovered in this rather wacky first kitchen designed for Sam Chesterton.

In almost all civilized societies where the resources are available for well-planned and sophisticated houses, the kitchen forms the focal point of everyday existence, excluding the very rich or those living in institutions. American and European culture is similar in this respect. In every European country there are examples, dating back to the Middle Ages, of the underlying concept of the sociable kitchen. The medieval great hall was a multi-purpose space centred around the cooking and eating of food, although perhaps as the warmest place in the castle many would also sleep there. Later on in the eighteenth and nineteenth centuries in Scandinavia, tiled stoves, found in many kitchens, had specially designed sleeping spaces around the chimney breast, especially in the poorer homes, although by

Lutyens' only design for a small comfortable kitchen — at Lindisfarne Castle in Northumberland — was way ahead of its time. This was because it was intended for use not only by the staff but also by its owners — a prerequisite for a comfortable kitchen.

OPPOSITE
This close-up of the stove in the kitchen at Erddig illustrated on page 31 shows examples of the various pots and pans used in such grand houses.

the late nineteenth century this practice had ceased. The link to the hearth gave the kitchen a pivotal position in our households. Today this is symbolic but still has a powerful effect on our attitude to the kitchen.

The sociable role of the kitchen adapts to its cultural and functional requirements. In the last thirty years it has undergone substantial changes. In Anglo-Saxon cultures before 1945 the kitchen was not a room in which visitors would be received or generally where relaxing or social activities would take place, except perhaps in some rural areas where the farmhouse kitchen, now seen as our main kitchen-role model, never died. By the late 1980s the kitchen had become for most households a dining room too and that meant a major social role. If you add some kind of soft space, such as a sofa or carpet, then you are including the sitting room function also.

In August 1980 *The Sunday Times* published a story entitled 'Why This Awful Fixation With Fitted Kitchens' explaining my basic ideas. The response was enthusiastic; around 2,000 enquiries resulted within a short period of time. From the response I was aware that I could not supply enough kitchens to meet the demand. Some years later I approached

Elizabeth David's main kitchen in the years from 1980 to 1991 was the antithesis to the fitted kitchens of the period. Her stove was free-standing and her equipment was stored on dressers, plate racks and simple pegs drilled into the wall.

Smallbone who enthusiastically took up the concept in 1987, by which time I had developed the unfitted kitchen more fully. Production drawings and manufacturing techniques were devised along with prototypes and training manuals for sales staff. The furniture was built to order and had over a thousand variations. There were many new ideas in the collection. The most radical was that the units, or counters, were not expected to fit wall-to-wall, turning current practice on its head. Corners are key architectural features and there was to be space where possible around each piece of furniture. The planning concept was based on the idea of dedicated work areas. Long runs of worktops tend to be used more as shelves, so the worktops were generally restricted to around the length of two out-stretched elbows, about 4 ft (1.38 metres). Worktop materials and heights were varied to suit different activities.

Large-scale storage is best provided by floor-to-ceiling cupboards, not interrupted and dispersed by a gap between a worktop and a wall-mounted, eye-level cupboard where the depth is reduced by half. Several cupboards were designed for this collection, including the court cupboard and parlour cupboard. Many other new types of furniture were developed (see chapters 3, 4 and 6) to accommodate the idea that a kitchen needed to be furnished with normal free-standing furniture like another room and was ostensibly a sociable room, not just a working kitchen.

It seems that we have gone a full circle and that the new sociable kitchen is very close to the kitchen-as-house model of earlier times, but with the addition in our contemporary home of well-serviced private rooms for sleeping and bathing. The public rooms have stayed too, but with a diminished role. Who knows what the future might bring as the fashions and uses of rooms merge and change, but I would be surprised if the ascendancy of the sociable kitchen is challenged in the foreseeable future.

A Visual History

THE SEVENTEENTH CENTURY –
THE IDEA OF COMFORT

The pursuit of comfort is the underlying force for change in domestic life. The meaning of the word has altered and developed dramatically. John Lukac wrote in 'The Bourgeois Interior', *American Scholar*, Vol. 39, No. 4, that until words such as self-confidence, self-esteem and sentimentality appear, then 'comfort' – the full appreciation of the feelings of self – is not possible. These words did not appear in the English or French language until between the sixteenth and seventeenth centuries.

What is the essence of comfort, the goal of most individuals in their pursuit of the perfect house? The word 'comfortable' comes from the Latin root *confortare*, meaning to console, support, strengthen or invigorate. According to the *Shorter Oxford English Dictionary* in the 1725 edition, it was defined as 'strengthening or supporting', in the 1748 edition 'affording

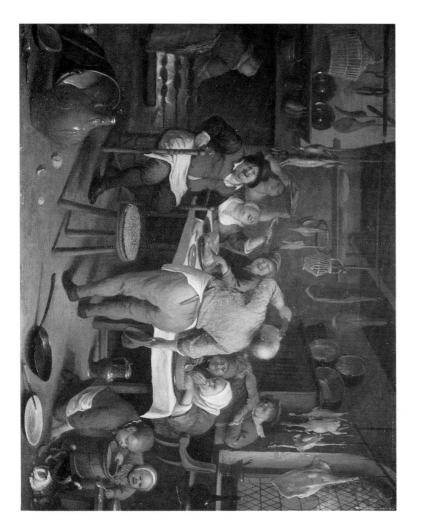

The woman tending the open range is seemingly ignoring the boisterous crowd round the table in this simple seventeenth-century Dutch kitchen scene, painted by Jan Havicksz Steen.

This Dutch seventeenth-century painting by Gillis van Tilborg of a noble family dining shows the extent to which family life in the Netherlands for the privileged was advanced in terms of comfort. This is evident in the small scale of the room, the quality of furniture, paintings, clothes, silver and gold plate, drinking glasses and the presence of children and dogs.

pleasure or delight' was added, and in the 1769 edition the word was further amplified as 'fitted to give tranquil enjoyment and content', also 'free from pain and trouble'. The starkness of medieval interiors with their lack of comfort reflected the bareness of people's inner lives. So there seems to be a clear connection.

Life was a public affair with little sense of or need for privacy or inner life. A great deal of activity was performed unselfconsciously because there was little separation between ceremony and utility, with the former dominating everything from the position in the household to even simple functions like washing hands and the choice of clothes to wear. Ceremony implies becoming part of a process not as an individual but as part of a group where preordained tradition makes for the ego to be subordinated. All objects, including household equipment, had a meaning and a place in life. There was no such thing as pure function according to Witold Rybcznski in his book *Home*, 'We may be able to separate function from beauty, age or style today, but in medieval times there was no such distinction.' Their thinking would have been based on pagan or early Christian ideas where superstition and an omnipotent preordained

This corner of what is probably
a large kitchen in a Dutch
seventeenth-century painting by
Jan Javicksz indicates perfect
balance between comfort and the
utilitarian demands of a living
kitchen. The wall space is used
for hanging a mixture of
practical objects, pictures and
plates.

22

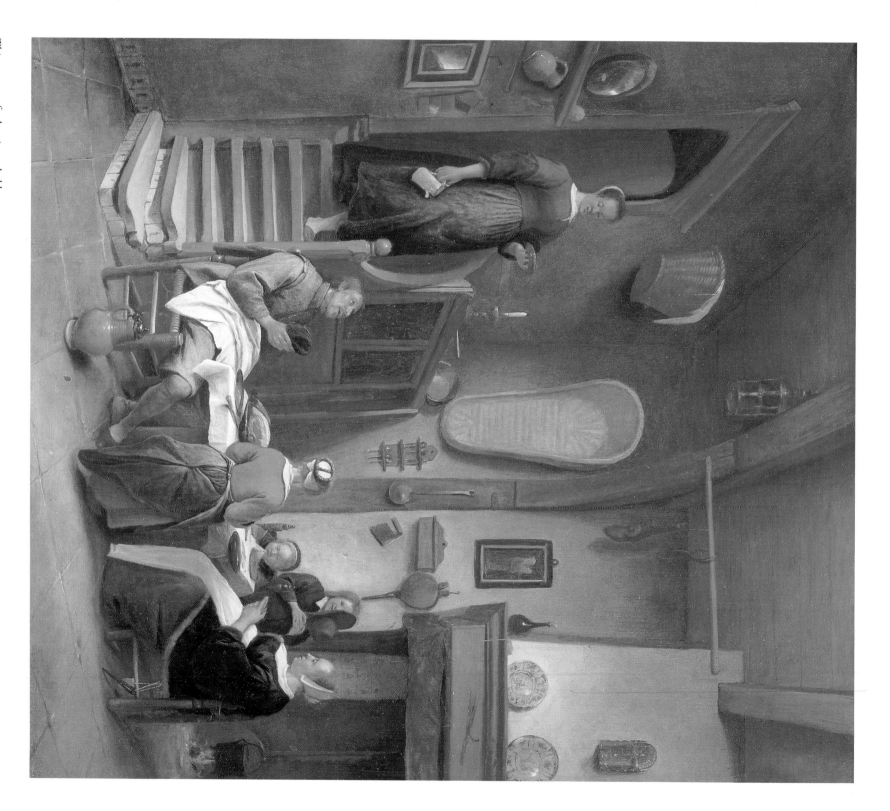

universe explained how the world worked. Ideas of personal comfort could not develop until the individual and ego had more status, and it is an interesting connection that with the development of an inner life for man, a domestic interior or inner life to match, also emerges according to John Lukac. Well-off medieval families could have easily afforded specialized rooms but had no concern to do so. That the resources were available is shown in their finely carved furniture, tapestries, and the beautifully made gold, silver and pewter utensils which adorned their tables.

By the seventeenth century the modern idea of domestic comfort started to take shape in northern Europe, particularly in the Netherlands which was the 'Japan' of her time, and around the cities of the Hanseatic League. With little land or resources the Netherlands had become an advanced, prosperous trading nation; no longer an agrarian society, it was the first European country where bourgeois values ruled. Small neatly planned houses were built, with an emphasis on domestic life. The Calvinist religion advocated simplicity and thrift. Family life was extremely precious to the Dutch merchants who prized their children above all,

Hendrick Martensz Sorgh's early seventeenth-century painting shows peasants merry-making in a humble kitchen. Despite being somewhat primitive – chickens are scratching at the earth floor – it still looks inviting and is reasonably spacious, although probably a little cold in winter.

An excellent example of a typical Dutch bourgeois kitchen of the late seventeenth century — spacious, well-planned, well-lit, ordered and pragmatic — is given in Gillis de Winter's painting. The dresser shelves display valuable pewter plates and spoons, a sign of prosperity. The food cupboard, designed to keep food off the damp floor and away from vermin, is typical of its time.

followed by their house and garden. According to *Daily Life in Rembrandt's Holland* by Paul Zumthov, 'The kitchen was the most important part promoted to a position of fantastic dignity and became something between a temple and a museum.'

One reason for this was that the ground floor rooms of these Dutch houses were often high, making a generous, well-ventilated and well-lit elegant space. The chimney breast, constructed out of stone with carved details, dominated the layout. (The rest of the house would probably be of timber construction.) A series of items of finely made free-standing and built-in furniture, the main pieces of which would be a large food cupboard, with a semi-display dresser to show off their highly prized pewter-ware plates, spoons, utensils and jugs, furnished the kitchen. There was also a variety of small tables (probably portable) for working at, large barrels for use both as worktops and as storage containers, presumably for storing water, ale, wine and dried goods; hanging racks for keeping meat away from vermin and dogs; a collection of additional pieces of portable furniture, such as pews, tables and chairs; large copper containers for washing dishes and possibly even a purpose-built sink if a hand pump had been installed in the room. The first hot water 'tanks' date from this time.

The taming or civilizing of the kitchen came about because the mistress of the household was closely involved herself. There were servants, but she carried out many of the household chores herself. The women's position and influence in society were greatly increased. Domesticity, a relatively new idea according to John Lukac's book, was 'prominently a feminine achievement' and linked to the increasing attempt to create and understand the idea of comfort. It is the creation of a home which means more than a house or a palace; a home is a sanctuary encompassing love, contentment, family life and nourishment – both of the body and mind. In his book entitled *Home*, Witold Rybcznski says it represents more a 'state of being' and has no equivalent in Latin or Slavic European languages. Danish, Swedish, German, Dutch and English all have similar-sounding words derived from the old Norse 'heima'.

The extreme conditions of winter caused the development of the first enclosed stand-up stoves not only in the Netherlands but also in Scandinavian countries. Warmth was at a premium and only one room could be reliably or fully heated during the depth of winter. Invariably the kitchen became the place where most family life took place. Children and servants probably slept in the kitchen, and as happened for several centuries later in rural properties in Europe, baths took place there too. These early, sociable one-room 'house-kitchens' developed by the early nineteenth century into civilized well-designed kitchens much in advance of other countries. The

Wine bottles are cooling in a copper container on the floor in Pierre Angelis' painting of elegant merrymakers. Pewter plates are displayed on the dresser.

Scandinavians today have a good design sense which combines a practical eye with no-nonsense comfort, which is derived from a domestic tradition that is probably linked to these early roots.

It seems that the tradition of the sociable kitchen is connected with the more prosperous rural families and hard-working bourgeoisie in towns where a mixture of circumstances required a pragmatic, well-organized household that was sufficiently affluent to allow for the luxury of basic comforts but where the families actively used their kitchens and did not rely on an army of servants. This provides us with a parallel for today, except the servants are machines. For hard-working families now especially if both parents work, a separate space for 'relaxing' is unlikely to be satisfactory.

THE EIGHTEENTH AND EARLY
NINETEENTH CENTURIES –
THE SPREAD OF CIVILIZED VALUES:
PRIVACY, BEAUTY AND ELEGANCE

The civilized ideas coming from the bourgeoisie of the Netherlands were ahead of their time, but well suited to the Age of Reason. The eighteenth century lay claim to being enlightened. In England it was an age 'of liberty and the rule of law, creative vigour in all trades and arts that serve and adorn man', according to G. M. Trevelyan in *An Illustrated English Social History*. He continues that it was 'a society with an outlook of its own, self-poised, self-judged, freed from the disturbing passions of the past and not yet troubled with anxieties of a very different future which was soon to be brought upon the scene by the industrial and French revolutions'.

The development of the idea of comfort has two strands in this century. Its pragmatic side belonged to the Dutch and English Georgian traditions, but the other side – the new 1748 definition (as given in the *Shorter Oxford Dictionary*), affording 'pleasure or delight' – belongs to the French and their rococo 'interiors'.

Households were now smaller without the public character of the 'open-plan' medieval house. The number of rooms for separate purposes ensured more privacy and the atmosphere of the house altered. The

The grand, elegant lady, accompanied by her child and maid, depicted by Antoine Raspal, shows how far domestication of the kitchen had spread in France by the late eighteenth century. Unlike her forbears who would have eschewed the kitchen, she works in this cramped, over-used space with its bread oven at the rear, storage furniture, solid worktops on masonry piers and tall fireplace.

The raised hearth shown in this mid-eighteenth-century painting by Johan Daniel Bager was a great improvement to cooking over coals on the floor.

change in attitude towards children, the smaller rooms and reduced need for protection against marauding intruders compared to earlier times meant that family life developed a sense of intimacy.

In France with the accession of Louis XV to the throne in 1715, formality and grandeur were replaced by what is termed the rococo style – it expressed such qualities as intimacy, elegance, a sense of fun. It was the first genuine decorative style in the sense that there was an element of fashion to it. The invention of sprung upholstery and the design of comfortable, ergonomic seating exemplified a huge improvement in not only the technical skill of master craftsmen such as Poppleman, Cuvilliés and Chippendale, but also the attitudes of architects to the creation of well-ordered, elegant interiors and the increasing interest in science and technology.

It is interesting that some major architects such as the Adam brothers were more involved in (and probably better at) designing interiors than the outside of buildings. Although the rococo style had faded as a cultural influence in Europe by the 1770s when the Adam brothers were at their zenith, it left behind the idea that comfort was not just heroic elegance as previously, but more that it had a light-heartedness in which pleasure, even pandering a little towards self-indulgence and cosiness, was expressed. This was the first time that grand interiors had descended into the depths of intimate personal comfort. The attitudes gained at the pinnacle of society percolated through and affected all levels. The rococo 'style', Osbert Lancaster wrote in *Here of All Places*, was 'the discovery of a way to reconcile fashion and comfort', but it was more. He went on, 'It is far rather a way of feeling a mood which may recur in any sufficiently sophisticated epoch.' It probably was the first example of a set of ideas that could be described as a furnishing style and it is nonetheless interesting and enriching for that.

Inevitably, by the time the classical revival eclipsed the rococo style, the widespread interest in classical antiquity had spread to most intellectual areas of the arts. The rococo joie-de-vivre gave way to the well-ordered formality of classicism. However, outbreaks of frivolity crept through in the classic revival especially later on with variants inspired by Egyptology and the influences of ancient Rome, Gothic, Chinese and Moorish cultures.

The Brighton Pavilion, built by the Prince Regent, is a clear example of rococo outbreak in the midst of a 'classical' period. The kitchen there is particularly interesting as an example of attitudes to architectural aspects, to the technical advances with cooking equipment, such as cast-iron ranges, to ventilation and light, and to its sense of order and aesthetic qualities. Although a 'commercial' kitchen, it was nevertheless given priority by the Prince Regent and considered the most modern and elegant kitchen in Europe at the time. The palm tree columns were hardly

ABOVE

The new interest in ventilation, light and efficient cooking, exemplified in John Nash's painting of Brighton Pavilion, had a big impact on commercial and domestic kitchen design in the nineteenth century. It was functional but also stylish. Good facilities were one way of persuading highly valued, chefs to stay.

BELOW

George Walker depicts a woman making oatcakes in a more humble Yorkshire kitchen where ingenuity and making-do with the existing furniture were demanded.

OPPOSITE
The kitchen at Erddig in Wales has all the hallmarks of a strong classical design. Built in 1772, it is subject to an extreme architectural discipline but remains elegant and simple, elevating the kitchen through its formal composition to the same importance as other rooms in the house.

'undecorated'. A new sense of decorum was arriving in the kitchen. The design would have been known about and had an impact on, for example, the kitchen at Erddig.

For the majority though, the kitchen probably remained tied to a large open-hearth with its attendant smoke and inefficiency. Thomas Robinson designed the first cast-iron range in 1780. It was similar to a domestic hob grate of the period but had an oven on one side and a hot water chamber on the other. George Bodley in 1802 patented an enclosed kitchen range which, although open-framed, had a cast-iron top to accommodate cooking pots and pans more efficiently. These ranges would have been installed in any 'modern' kitchen of the period and would have had a tremendous impact on the speed and ease of cooking. Count Rumford made his contribution in the 1770s using scientific principles to understand the design of efficient stoves, but his ideas were ignored for another hundred years. Until the 1900s improved versions of the Robinson stove were common. So the kitchen stove with its exposed fire box continued to be the most reliable hearth, its comforting aspect a major draw for domestic activity. An open fire is companionable too, especially in the absence of friends or domestic activity. A table was always nearby, whether in use for eating or for food preparation, and, as continued well into the twentieth century in pubs, a high-backed settle or straw beehive chair — traditional to Wales and Scotland — to keep draughts out stood on one side of the fire.

Towards the end of this period the separation of activities into different rooms had begun in many well-off homes and even in some modest rural dwellings where a scullery for washing clothes, washing up and some food preparation was created. Certainly in prosperous farmhouses there would have been a 'wet' kitchen. Depending on local traditions there would also have been a pantry, dairy, brewhouse, smokehouse and outside storerooms for specialist produce.

For the poor, mere survival was all that they could achieve. Their possessions were few and furniture was a luxury. Theirs is a separate story from the discourse in the mainstream of this book, but they are affected by the intellectual climate of society as a whole. During the eighteenth century the population of England nearly doubled, mostly due to people living longer because of advances in medical and scientific knowledge. Improved agricultural techniques and relatively full employment resulted in better nourishment. The revolution in rural life through the Enclosure Acts worked, to quote G. M. Trevelyan, 'by the creation of a new order not by an expansion of an old economic system. Great compact estates, cultivated in large farms by leasehold tenants, covered more acreage at the expense of various forms of petty cultivation.' This ensured a prosperous yeoman farming class during the following century; it is they who form the strongest model for our sociable kitchen — the so-called farmhouse

The Georgian aesthetic was exported around the world, particularly to the colonies and the United States. It became an international style. Here its language is clearly on display, its adaptability to grand or humble dwellings and to architectural fittings or furniture. The effects of this truly remarkable set of aesthetic guidelines are clearly visible in this kitchen at Hancock Shaker Village.

kitchen. It was in the cities where the newly rich bourgeois classes and aristocratic intellectuals lived, that the classical revival started to develop its peculiar English identity towards the end of the eighteenth century.

The newly separated public rooms of the house – the drawing room, dining room and library – began to take on new character. The dining room became a male-dominated room, the drawing room larger and more under feminine influence. The furniture became more comfortable, changing the latter room from being a grand salon into a series of small independent groupings of furniture rather than pieces being placed around the perimeter of the room and being linked into the architectural design. The library became more of a family room, less formal and used for family get-togethers and not as a silent study. Furniture was chosen and arranged in a more casual way. A more 'natural' way of furnishing started to develop, a precursor to a 'modern' expressive way of furnishing, showing the beginnings of a romantic movement which flowered in the late nineteenth century. The development of the character of these three rooms – the dining room, library and drawing room – affects the design of

the kitchen today – they are the blueprint for the public rooms we envisage when we imagine a normal or well-planned house today. The contemporary sociable kitchen has elements of all these rooms in its make-up.

Certainly the 'Georgian' house had a massive impact on European and American domestic architecture. The more relaxed planning meant irregularity, rather than rigid formality and found a more easily used format for domestic dwellings. Freer planning meant rooms could be changed in size, windows no longer needed to be imposed by outside architectural considerations, and if not positioned for inside convenience, then at least could be modified to suit interior requirements. Georgian design reconciled, to quote Praz in *Interior Decoration*, bourgeois practicality with 'fantasy and common sense with refinement'. Chippendale himself at the beginning of one of his pattern books, hoped his designs were 'elegant and useful'. That's just another way of describing 'comfort'.

England was the dominant force in European politics and world trade at the time these ideas spread. The growing American middle classes related well to the comfort of Georgian design and it was adopted via cabinetmakers and builders' guides. American Chippendale, for example, lasted longer than in England and became the basis for the all-American colonial 'style'.

Clearly the Georgian style is adaptable and both 'high' and 'low church' is possible. Country-style solid wood furniture is equally much of the Georgian spirit as a more sophisticated, highly veneered bureau bookcase with inlay and carving. The wide variety of options and its flexibility to adapt to a wide range of different circumstances both in architectural construction or to suit specific interior decor, make it the first genuine 'international' style and probably one of the few successful ones. It has a strong homogenous element in Anglo-Saxon culture in the visual arts. For many architects and designers having seen the confusion and over-ornateness of nineteenth-century design, it remains a pure unadulterated aesthetic that set standards for an ideal design language, balancing both function, ease and comfort.

THE VICTORIAN AGE –
TECHNOLOGY AND REVIVALISM

Steering a course through influences on architecture and interior design in the nineteenth century is hazardous. The attempt to dress the inventions of the time in traditional costume within a multiplicity of historical revivalist styles implies a lack of confidence in their own era but is misplaced. The sheer speed of technological advancement, population expansion, political change and growth of cities, were more easily absorbed by using historical pastiche and traditional forms. Even if it was only superficial, it helped with acceptance of change and new technology. The first trains were designed as a horse carriage look-alike (although the engine itself proved harder to masquerade as a horse); certainly the 'carriages' showed little difference from their horse-drawn forebears.

The advances in technology in Britain at any rate were matched by social advances through the rise in humanitarianism, softening the brutality of the past but at times spilling over into sentimentality, a factor so evident in Victorian interiors which helps to explain one of the causes of revivalism. Charles Dickens' books reflected all these qualities, including the self-help protestant work ethic that provided such a stimulus to Victorian industrial success. The irony is that it drove the middle classes to flee from it in their homes and hence their interiors as

A nineteenth-century painting by Franz Wieschebrink of a mid-European kitchen shows an interesting range made in cast-iron. It seems to be about 6ft (1.8 metres) long with a tall central section which was used as a bread oven as well as a rack to dry boots. There is nothing like baking to bring family members into the kitchen!

a kind of sanctuary to create a self-selected reality, epitomized by the amount of ephemera hung on the walls, by the resurrected Gothic style and its semi-religious atmosphere, and through the escape into the romantic movement and a newly invented rusticity exemplified by the arts and crafts movement.

For the well-off it was a more comfortable world with technology assisting in many areas from heating, a ready supply of furniture and building materials, through to servants, many of whose families had been expelled from the land by the Enclosure Acts. It was the steady rise of puritan religious values that made family life more formal during the middle decades of the century. The kitchen was not the comfortable centre of the house – for that you had to go to the parlour or library. However, for the servants themselves the below-stairs kitchen had its own comfort, not least of all through the shared companionship of labour in the wealthier houses.

For those in-between classes, for many rural middle classes and those in similar positions in France, Italy and America, the kitchen remained the centre of the home, especially if shorn of its laundry and peripheral activities. Many household goods that were previously made at home could now be purchased from shops and mail order catalogues, ranging from soap and shoe polish, to string, matches and cooking utensils, although for the poor affording these would have been difficult. The extra-curricular activities in the kitchen were starting to be reduced.

This kitchen in a grand house, as depicted by Frank Watkins in 1875, seems to have a plethora of chopping blocks and copper pans. The tall cupboard in the centre of the picture is intriguing because it appears so awkwardly placed and without a panelled back. All the other furniture is carefully made and ornately detailed.

With self-respect and ingenuity a small kitchen can be made to work for you. This Glasgow tenement kitchen often doubled as a bedroom for a grandparent, maid or younger child. The warmth, particularly in winter when it may have been the only warm room in the house, compensated for the lack of privacy, addressed by installing curtains.

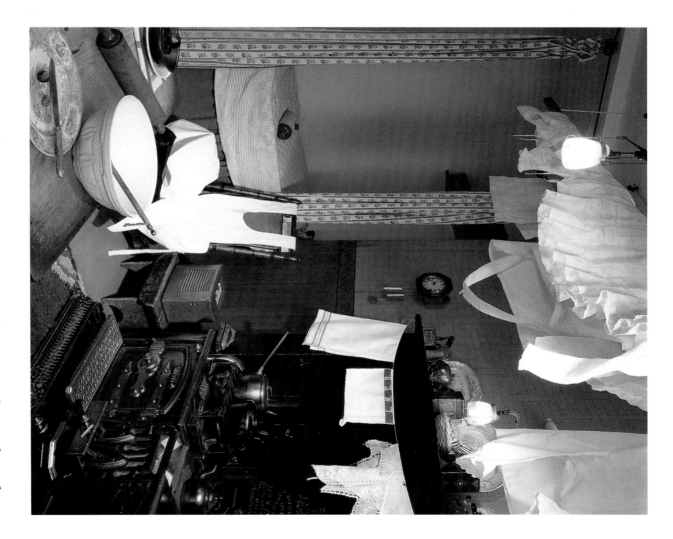

Being poor did not necessarily mean abandoning any hope of comfort. Each individual, depending on past experience, whether from rural or city background, had different expectations and ideas of comfort. The Glasgow tenement block kitchen, although tiny by our standards, still offered the chance of hard-earned comfort, of being surrounded by an extended family within sight of a hearth with a meal on the table. Accompanied by hope, even basic surroundings that are familiar, cared for and with a good family atmosphere can be comfortable. The doctrine of self-help, accompanied by opportunity in education and the wider society of work and trade, makes the physically small domestic space seem bigger.

The gypsy caravan, a nineteenth-century invention, a tiny all-purpose room on wheels where every square inch was utilized, rendered no ill-effects to its proud occupants, quite the reverse in fact. The lives of gypsies depended on the outside, the countryside providing their fare. Comfort is in the head as well as in the backside! Both needs have to be met, one being internal and the other external.

The pace of change in the Victorian age and people's fascination with technology must have generated a great feeling of optimism; doubly so in the New World where individuals had the chance to achieve unlimited self-improvement which is a major element in the pioneering spirit. Exploration, literally reaching out to new frontiers, drove the Victorian age into a self-generating rampage for new products, new ideas and change.

The American interest in efficiency in housework was led by women, amongst whom was Catherine Beecher, who wrote a remarkable treatise on domestic economy in 1849. Her book centred not on style but convenience. She focused for the first time in history on the idea of an efficient, easy-to-maintain home. She discussed the kitchen in detail, suggesting a planned relationship between the sink and the stove, new ideas for storage

Marcel Proust spent his holidays with his Aunt Léonie. This unassuming kitchen under the labours of her resident cook, Françoise, produced food that for Proust had the status of art and inspired him to write his great work 'Remembrance of Things Past'.

of towels and a form of scouring powder, and proposing the stove should be separated by glass doors from the rest of the room to keep the air clean. (Victorians were obsessed by change of 'air' and ventilation.)

Catherine Beecher accepted that the work was to be done by women, but these young American housekeepers did not have the servants their European counterparts had and therefore would be direct beneficiaries of an efficient easy-to-manage 'home'. According to Witold Rybczsnski, the earlier masculine idea of the home – the European gentleman's house – was as a sanctuary and a male reserve. She put forward the feminine idea of the home as dynamic: 'It was to do with ease and work. It could be said to have shifted the focus from the drawing room to the kitchen.' These ideas, revolutionary at the time, are much closer to the modern concept of a home and represent a huge change from contemporaneous thinking.

Interestingly, she was concerned about the labour of caring for a big house and suggested a smaller house because the care and use of it could be more comfortable. The disadvantage of a large house meant that 'the table furniture, the cooking materials and utensils, the sink, the eating room are at such distances apart that half the time and strength is employed in walking back and forth to collect and return articles used'. American classless society was readier to cope with new ideas on the social front and was ahead of its time, but England followed eventually towards the acceptance of smaller houses, especially after the First World War as women were emancipated through their war work.

When the working area of the Victorian kitchen, cooking stove apart, was performing its role in feeding a large household, it showed improved organization over its eighteenth-century counterpart. More furniture was

Frederick Daniel Hardy's mid-nineteenth-century painting of this domestic kitchen scene is an evocation of a simple rural life devoid of frills. At the near right-hand corner stands the copper where all the water was heated for laundry and bathing. Furniture was a scarce luxury for many, apart from stools and the odd table and cupboard. Kitchen furniture such as dressers were a sign of prosperity.

built in, larger central preparation tables were built, greater cleanliness and order prevailed. The wider availability of all types of cooking utensils and equipment, ironmongery, crockery and china is evident in the painting of Mrs Cartwright's kitchen at Langton Hall, Aynho . . . a food mincer (a recent invention) attached to the wall; better lighting from an oil chandelier; a variety of teapots and jelly moulds (the Victorians must have been obsessed with jelly judging by the voluminous presence in almost every nineteenth-century kitchen I have ever seen) and the extensive bain marie hot plates provided in the range, heated by charcoal presumably, below the window. Already the presence of tall decorated purpose-made dressers was giving signs that a display of possessions was necessary to show the family position or status since the room had a public face (to visitors). The kitchen was 'furnished' and not just a place of work.

A kitchen in a less affluent household would certainly have shown more personal signs of occupation. Since earliest times crockery, eating utensils, chinaware and so on have been more personal than mere pieces of equipment. We are 'connected' to our stomachs in many subtle ways — by possessions, technology, architecture, agriculture, social attitudes, necessity and the sheer pleasure of eating. All of which were affected by the passage of events of the nineteenth century.

The dialogue between two aspects of comfort show up here and not so much as outlined above as a 'class' proposition. Two poles of thought emerge, and are debated by Katherine Girier in her excellent book, *Culture and Comfort, People, Parlors and Upholstery*. Her book investigates the history of the American parlour where domesticity provides the basis for comfort, and culture represents the cosmopolitan or public face that the householder wishes to express. This is the mantle that the sociable kitchen of today takes on when absorbing the function of a public room in its dining and living room elements. Culture, according to Katherine Girier, is used as a 'shorthand for the cultivated world view of educated, genteel cosmopolitan people whose habits of consumption were intended to create expressive social demeanor'.

Comfort, she went on, 'signals a group of ideas and beliefs not simply associated with a pleasurable physical state. It designates presence of the more family-centered, even religious values associated with home, emphasizing perfect sincerity and moderation.' The creation of a home was at the core of the Victorian culture. It was a web of symbols, ideas, objects and images that were all powerful. To be at home is not just to be in residence but to be at ease in any company, good manners being part of this.

With such a strong cultural pressure it is not surprising that the desire for the perfect home, for comfort, signifying efficiency, and culture, signifying appropriateness and style, became such dominating forces in the twentieth century.

THE TWENTIETH CENTURY: EFFICIENCY AND COMFORT

Ergonomics, the method or science of measuring efficiency, was first applied to the home by Catherine Beecher in *A Treatise on Domestic Economy*, published in 1849 in the United States. With the aid of diagrams and photographs she explained how every aspect of housework, cooking included, could be made more efficient. The success of her book, combined with another entitled *The Homemaker and Her Job* by Lillian Gilbreth shortly afterwards, caused a rethinking of the concept of domestic comfort, initially in the United States, and later in Europe. Many of the ideas about kitchen planning that appear self-evident today, originated through the work of these two pioneers, from the height of the worktops, and the organization of storage, to the layout of the kitchen and even the size of houses. In 1914 Christine Frederick in her *Efficiency Studies in Home Management* proposed a servantless household, replacing ill-trained servant girls with machines and better planning.

Gilbreth advised her readers to organize their homes to their own work habits and to be guided by 'convenience not convention'. Her ideas must have been radical at the time; they have a pragmatism and optimism that is associated with American thinking, a freedom from old European traditions associated with social and domestic organization, that helps to explain why many twentieth-century design and furnishing trends come from the United States. New ideas have been taken up there with more enthusiasm, whether they relate to sociable kitchens or space technology.

SOCIABLE ROLE OF THE KITCHEN

RIGHT

Edith Hayllar's painting shows a typical English Edwardian country kitchen. Not much would have changed during the previous 100 years or so except the range is now a little more efficient and has a water heater. It still remains a comfortable and relaxing scene, even if lacking in the efficiencies of more modern kitchens.

OPPOSITE

Modernity arrives within an architectural framework in Edwin Lutyens' kitchen at Castle Drogo. The minimal palette of materials, simplicity of details, management of light and built-in nature of the furniture are forerunners of future trends in kitchen design.

The sturdy, pragmatic Scandinavian interest in good craftsmanship was easily adapted to Mackintosh arts and crafts influences from England, as this illustration by Carl Larsson shows. Design styles, particularly arts and crafts, happily cross national borders and often gain new life in the process. In the United States the popular mission style was developed from it.

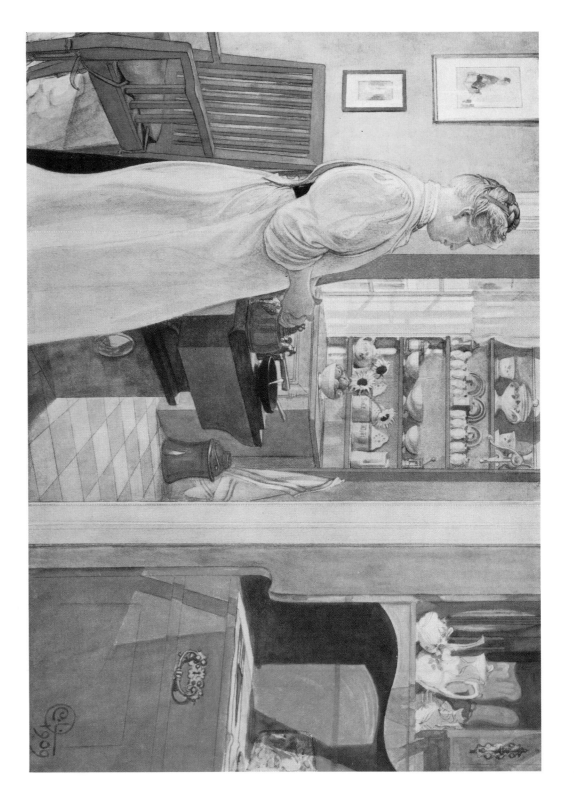

Decorative ideas and the comfort or cultural part of the equation though still came in abundant regularity from Europe with its long-standing traditions of craft and décor or 'style'. The arts and crafts movement, art deco and art nouveau, the Edwardian style, the neo-Tudor vernacular, the thirties deco, right up to the modern movement and post-modernism are all examples. As comfort relates also to cultural expression, it has the greater capacity to absorb human interest. The unchanging nature of ergonomics is associated with issues that are often technical, humdrum or certainly without 'expressive' qualities, so it is quite under-standable that style has become the focal point in many conversations about the kitchen.

This century has not only seen the speed of new cultural trends and styles accelerate, presumably because of the development of communica-tions and electronic media, but also the proliferation of styles inspired by local, sub-cultural or commercial interests, the latter being based on customer profiles and such like. They become popular if they reach major 'architectural' status as opposed to just 'furnishing' styles. Furniture-makers have been traditionally slow to take notice of new styles; until the

Protect your family's health
Clean the refrigerator with Old Dutch and
safeguard food with *Healthful Cleanliness*

Most kitchens in the United States had refrigerators by the early 1930s. American housewives were urged to safeguard their family's health by using special cleansers.

This beautiful detail is of the kitchen at the Gamble House in Pasadena, California, by Greene & Greene who were inspired by arts and crafts principles of integrity in their design of interior spaces; the simplicity and control of the woodwork is awe-inspiring yet also calming.

big kitchen manufacturers developed after the Second World War, they assumed furniture was destined for a long life and therefore not subjected to short-term fashions. The bigger kitchen manufacturers can, by adopting a high-profile advertising campaign, now even create their own new 'style' which is frequently based on spurious claims of originality with little aesthetic integrity or coherence.

It is hard to see where all this profusion of 'styles' takes us, except perhaps back to a point before mass-communications where locally inspired traditions allow for some continuity and an attempt to show integrity and honesty in expression – a conclusion that William Morris arrived at and which forms the philosophical basis of the arts and craft movement that flourished in the second half of the nineteenth century. The architects Voysey, Mackintosh and Greene & Greene in the United States, and furniture-makers such as Godwin, Lethaby, Sir Ambrose Heal and Morris himself, were all influenced by these ideas. It is interesting that Morris essentially used furniture-making as his prime form of expression and his search for truth. His concern with the use of appropriate materials, simplicity, hand-work and rural traditions, and his dislike of veneers and ornament had an almost puritanical flavour which still influences us today in our attitude to design and craftsmanship. In the United States, mission and Shaker furniture remains perennially popular, its austerity widely admired, likewise with arts and crafts period furniture in England. All were attempts at creating both a sense of order and aesthetic 'honesty' in our furniture and interiors.

In his own way Le Corbusier, one of the most influential architect-philosophers of this century, tried to make the designing of houses more efficient and less emotionally self-indulgent, like Frederick and Gilbreth before him. His skills stopped at the level of house construction and he did not consider house work in terms of efficiency; Europe had not reached advanced American ideas in domestic house planning with their larger homes, combined living rooms, built-in closets, shower baths, pantries, large refrigerators, washing machines and plentiful use of cheap kitchen labour-saving gadgets. During the fifties the impact of the confident American streamlining style, which probably emanated from the work of Raymond Loewy, on kitchen equipment was immense. This brazen aesthetic actually stemmed from the thirties and worked tremendously well as propaganda for the importance of 'modernity'. Partly because it was an 'expressive' style, it eventually became too style-obsessed and gave way to the quieter modernity of the seventies and the ubiquitous fitted kitchen with built-in appliances which originated in post-war Germany. As these trends began to take hold, the kitchen was propelled into the last phase of its move towards total austerity and efficiency, before finally reverting to incorporate the necessary comfort or sociable part of the equation in making the most important domestic space.

The liveliness of the kitchen in the eighties and nineties is Anglo-American inspired. The sociable or unfitted kitchen fits well into our cultural life. The English have a great tradition of small homes (as far as kitchens are concerned), with unselfconscious, slightly shabby but comfortable domestic interiors and a tolerance of unmatching furniture and quirky objects. Americans have larger homes and are a little more concerned with efficiency — but also with comfort. Comfort means space, useability and service (often considered as an American invention). And comfort means to cosset yourself — perhaps a little bit of self-indulgence which in earlier times was provided by the hearth; in the kitchen of today it comes from the furniture and surroundings. I suspect this sums up current contemporary aspirations in both the United States and England.

What has the twentieth century given us that is new in terms of attitudes towards comfort and efficiency? In terms of efficiency, science and technology clearly provided us at the beginning of the period with a grandiose optimism that they could solve all our problems. By the end of the century we have realized their limits. The human factor and the replacement of scientific determinism with the 'chaos' theory have shown that order and disorder live together; science is not reductionism but the study of the whole and is a state of becoming, not being. 'Chaotic' dynamics, according to James Gleick in his book Chaos, discovered that disorderly behaviour of simple systems acted as a creative process. Translated into solving the problems of modern living, this means that we have

OPPOSITE

The fitted-kitchen concept originated in Germany but was swiftly taken up in the United States. It reduced the kitchen to a manufacturer's idea of convenience and efficiency, and was devoid of clutter or humanity.

The earliest American built-in kitchen furniture was co-ordinated with an appliance. Streamlined and easy to clean, but also cold, repetitive and sterile, it lacked any inviting aspects that create a room in which to dwell, eat or conduct family life.

The advertisement for Hotpoint, published in Life magazine, conveys the rapid pace of technological advance in the early 1950s.

AND NOW! FABULOUS "FOODARAMA" BY KELVINATOR!

166-lb. Upright Freezer, and an 11 cu. ft. "Moist Cold" Refrigerator, both in a cabinet only 47 inches wide

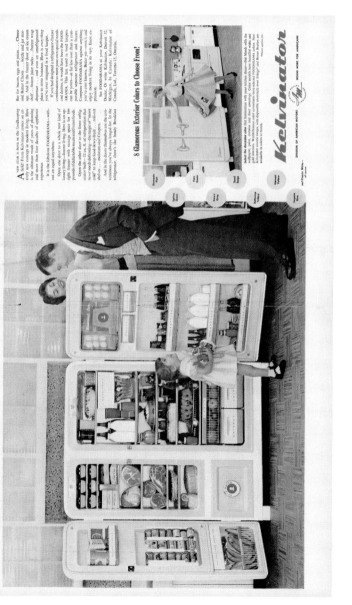

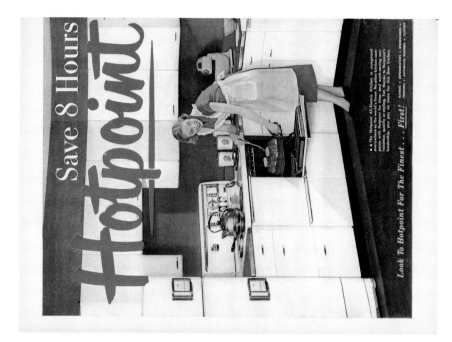

This detail of the Castle Drogo kitchen by Lutyens shows architectural fittings placed in alcoves and a free-standing circular table which is thoroughly modern in flavour, and advanced in its controlled aesthetic.

bypassed the idea of machines to live in – the mere 'functional' provision of physiological needs is not enough. Human beings need the so-called 'irrational' clutter of human life that puritan modernists thought was superfluous. To everyday ephemera, art objects and consumer products such as kitchen crockery, we attach 'emotional' meaning. It is part of building up a 'cultural ego', a network of intellectual and emotional attitudes, a kind of metaphysical cocoon that provides us with a way of thinking about ourselves and how we intend others to perceive us.

The selection of these everyday objects as social status markers is now understood. In the *World of Goods, Towards an Anthropology of Consumption*, Mary Douglas and Baron Isherwood showed how material possessions are used as a communication system, a code of transactions to say things about ourselves to the outside world. Understanding what drives consumption helps us to see what constitutes a 'comfortable' home, how 'style' or objects connect with us.

Each room of the house, the kitchen included, is a 'metaphorical' or non-physical extension of ourselves and for the visitor it is a helpful and fascinating guide to the personality of the family concerned. Being fully comfortable within your own home is being able to express your 'cultural ego' through the choice of objects. Being unable to do this – by living in rented accommodation, for example – causes a lack of comfort and certainly a lack of identification with your surroundings. The popularity of owner-occupation is testimony to that.

Another human aspect, the feminine and masculine balance of influence in the house, is now quite well resolved. The house is still a sanctuary, a fortress its 'male' element, but it is also a practical place with a feminine eye to efficiency. In the 'sociable' kitchen outlined in the

The kitchen table at Castle Drogo is a widely admired design, but it is technically flawed in its timber detailing. Large mitred joints shrink across their joins. Central heating is a hazard that has to be overcome in designing household furniture today. Central islands are now more sophisticated with many new demands, but the circular shape is practical, easy to live with and thoroughly challenging to make.

following chapters, the focus shifts more to a feminine 'dynamic' idea of the home. The resolving of the decor is a matter for each family or couple, together. By adding a 'soft' area and dining 'room', the kitchen becomes the predominant 'shared' room of the house.

Castle Drogo, designed by Lutyens, contains a kitchen which, although not a sociable kitchen as such, is a landmark in twentieth-century design. A clearly expressed plan, purpose-built without overtures to any particular style, it is a working kitchen that comprises a relatively few pieces of simply designed solid pieces of furniture. There is little mannerism in the design, few personal features or private artefacts, and a certain quality of serenity, probably derived from the management of light and minimal use of materials – the palette is local stone and limed oak. It is a 'modern' working kitchen well ahead of its time, more in terms of its style than in any claim to comfort.

The development of the fitted kitchen was an attempt to exemplify economic efficiency in the provision of the kitchen units and in their manufacture, marketing, distribution, and installation – not least in terms of cost. In such ways they were, and are, successful. In terms of comfort they are not.

The sociable kitchen attempts to work to a much wider brief: firstly on an architectural level reorganizing the house to fit an expanded role of the kitchen, secondly on a design level making maximum use of the space itself and the efficient execution of all intended activities, and thirdly on an individual level absorbing the cultural and more personal interests and ideas of the user into the design. The twentieth century ends with the resolving and re-interpretation of these themes as the main objective each time someone moves house or sets up a new home.

The current absence of one major cultural style or umbrella is, in my opinion, a benediction. One of the great advantages of being through what is known as the 'modern movement' or 'international style' is its purifying effect, cleansing the more excessive elements of nineteenth-century revivalism and its sentimentality. It was a puritanical movement and now that its heyday is over, the vacuum it left behind has created an unprecedented period of freedom of expression in design, architecture and home decoration. This may only last until another '...ism' becomes predominant, but it is welcome for those who enjoy individual expression and variety.

This unprecedented freedom is evident on all fronts, politically and domestically. We have to know how to exercise it to achieve a truly comfortable home and that is quite a challenge. The following chapters offer ideas and solutions that should help with meeting it.

2
CONTEMPLATING KITCHENS

Elizabeth David's Kitchens

The first visit I can recall to my aunt, Elizabeth David's house was at the age of five to receive instructions on how to cook a chicken! The extraordinary atmosphere of the kitchen was intensified by a wide range of exotic aromas from those dishes currently in preparation, as well as smells lingering from previous dishes, other fragrant spices, strong French cigarettes, and the various fruits on display. The room abounded with interesting objects, fascinating to a young child. The presence of three overladen dressers, a cramped main table and two smaller circular ones, two ancient cupboards, quite a few chairs and a chaise-longue allowed for plenty of parking surface for her many objects, both culinary and otherwise – and that didn't include a sink cabinet with generous draining boards.

The kitchen didn't seem peculiar to me. Our own one at home shared some of its features although it was a lot smaller. I enjoyed it because it was a bit like exploring a treasure chest. Mrs David, as she was affectionately called by the family, was equally fascinated by food and the objects connected with cooking and beyond. She talked to me as a child about her recent 'discoveries' and her interests without condescension – and with a lot of enthusiasm. I could not help but be interested. Later on when I was older, I realized that conversation was something she desired as she lived on her own. Although her sister Felicité lived upstairs, she worked in her bookshop during the day and they always rang each other up before invading the privacy of each other's part of the house, especially the kitchen because that was where Mrs David lived. Apart from early in the morning when she wrote in bed, the majority of her writing was done in the old kitchen. To all intents it was a study kitchen. More often than not when you called on her, books and papers were stacked on the table. When guests were invited to lunch, she would only have one dish ready, the ones to follow would be prepared over a lengthy pre-lunch conversation and guests were usually asked to assist at least in some minor way. All of this was done at the main table, with a scrubbed pine top. On occasions it received a tablecloth, but it was the working centre of the kitchen. She had no worktops as such.

All her recipes were thoroughly tested before being finally included in her manuscripts, and there were written notes, research books, peculiar new gadgets she was trying out and cooking equipment ever ready. If you

Elizabeth David's winter kitchen — designed by me in the early 1980s — shows the cupboard with sliding doors set at 2ft 3in (675 mm) from the ground — the most useful height for kitchen storage.

were lucky and some experiment had taken place the previous day, she would offer it to you in a matter-of-fact way and ask you to try it. Invariably it would be delicious. She never boasted about her cooking skills — her whole attitude to cooking was one of interest, enquiry and very occasionally genuine pleasure when a dish turned out well. Her emphasis on the quality of raw ingredients and on simplicity was evident in the kitchen — despite the clutter. The dresser that stood next to the entrance door always had an abundant collection of white bowls displaying her recent food purchases or gifts . . . semi-dried dates from California, Italian plum tomatoes, wild figs brought by a friend from Spain, giant yellow quinces from Greece and even free-range eggs piled up neatly. She owned a painting by Cedric Morris in which eggs are enchantingly arranged on an earthenware dish; it was used on the front cover of her anthology of writings, *An Omelette and a Glass of Wine*. Many other less exotic fruits of the season — humble things like walnuts, pears or shallots — were also in residence.

Mrs David complained about clutter in her kitchen but also realized that she would have to cope with it. Her curiosity in culinary objects and books was all-consuming and caused her to accumulate by default. The unlikely combination of a workshop, a large box room and an enormous

library that she needed to relieve her of it never came. Her kitchen filled in for their absence and the result was an extraordinary esoteric collection of fascinating objects, books and papers mixed with exotic smells and aromas.

Clutter there may have been, but in her mind she was highly organized. She had a brilliant memory, remembering names, books, paintings, poetry, dates, quotes and obscure details that gave her writing exceptional accuracy. She would notice items of interest that others missed. Walking down the street with her on a trip to Wales, I was constantly stimulated by her ability to spot unusual architectural details and her enjoyment of the unexpected. This gave her a particular interest in new ideas and demonstrated the independence of mind that accompanies this trait. She certainly had no desire for a streamlined, easy-to-clean fitted kitchen and took no notice of the social pressure for them, which was fairly extreme in the 1960s and 1970s.

She had spent many of her early years abroad and she was able to see how country people lived in France, Spain, Italy and Greece. So her idea of the kitchen was probably influenced by that experience. Certainly her own upbringing in a Sussex manor house with servants and a separate wing for children provided no role model or pleasing nostalgia. Her mother was definitely no cook and the nursery maid was responsible for the children's

The banquette designed by me for the winter kitchen. The First World War poster was found by her for reproduction in her bread encyclopedia, 'English Bread and Yeast Cookery'. The bag hanging on the chair was part of its promotion – an aspect she disliked. She was a private person who shunned publicity.

OVERLEAF

This view of the kitchen shows her work table and the early French 'armoire' used for storage of terracotta, Le Creuset and tin ware. The table was host to many hours of conversation and superb meals, as well as serving as her writing desk and food preparation surface.

The table and sink cabinet in the winter kitchen designed by me. Elizabeth David liked big china clay sinks in which she used two plastic bowls for the washing-up.

OPPOSITE

This early Georgian pine cupboard with sliding doors was used to store drinking glasses, carefully labelled spices from all over the world and a variety of exotic condiments and white coffee cups. The top surface housed a variety of large objects, partly chosen for their good looks.

food, not the cook. So the food did not exactly bring glowing memories. Perhaps it was as a compensation for this that she developed her interest in food. Her upstairs' kitchen was cobbled together with furniture selected for its functional and aesthetic offerings and was more akin to a study or sitting room than a kitchen. And why not? Certainly she planned it in an unconscious way, and as a pleasant place in which to live and work.

The sink cabinet that was already in place when she moved into her house in 1949 had more or less collapsed by 1979, so at her request I built her a new one in the street outside as soon as I left school. It was my first commission. I don't care to imagine what the neighbours thought about the shavings blowing down the street, although as far as I know she didn't have any comeback. I am not sure either how well it was put together, but it still stands. (I wish I had put a marble or slate upturn behind the sink, the present one is decidedly the worse for wear.) Anyway, she was appreciative and I ate some wonderful meals in exchange.

I suppose any criticism offered (although it's a little late, for she died in 1992) of the design of the kitchen, would be the need for better facilities

OPPOSITE
The dresser by the door, regarded as her best, dates from around the early 1800s. This housed fresh produce and interesting culinary objects like the French stainless steel madeleine biscuit moulds.

An assortment of heat diffusers and sieves hangs on pegs above the main kitchen stove.

around the stove and more heat-proof work space. Those gaps on either side of the stove were too small to clean easily. Mrs David did work tidily though, and always washed up as she went along. As it happens, I still remember that was the first lesson she taught me when I 'learned' how to cook that first chicken. It was also one of the duties of the guests to wash up after the meal was finished. She never had any staff and it was partly a matter of politeness and a way of saying thank you for a special meal.

There were clever touches in the kitchen. The use of a mirror placed just above worktop height by the Victorian dresser next to the stove effectively doubled the length of the dresser and had a subliminal effect on your appreciation of the size of the room. It gave that corner of the room a feeling of spaciousness and depth of interest.

Each dresser rack held a wide assortment of equipment and china. Earlier on in its life she displayed decorative china plates, but over the years decided that she preferred simple white china (mostly French) with less conspicuous display of decoration. She certainly loved the cooking utensils as much as the china and thought them equally worthy of display. Utilitarian objects intrigued her. Among her favourite shops were iron-mongers and we both had many interesting visits to them.

Her dislike of extraneous ornaments came to the fore when a manufacturer offered her a replacement stove. It had a lot of fussy extra dials and a plastic trim. She politely turned down the manufacturer's offer, consistent with her attitude when being offered a new cheese with herbs incorporated. 'When I want cheese with herbs in I'll do it myself, thank you.' To accompany her shopping was quite an experience.

By far the most beautiful piece of furniture in her kitchen was the French *armoire*, possibly as early as sixteenth century and coming from the Lyons district. This housed all her large pots and pans as well as her French and Spanish terracotta cooking dishes. She particularly liked dishes that were suitable for use both in the oven or on the hob and which could be transferred straight on to the table by placing them on a cool plate. This saved on washing up, as well as keeping the food hot. On the pegs above the stove she kept a number of different heat-spreading devices that allowed her to use terracotta without the heat cracking it. The early cast-iron Le Creuset pans fulfilled the same function and were other favourites of hers.

For food preparation apart from the washing of vegetables and so on, she again used the main table. For this purpose she kept a variety of cutting boards. A minute one was used for garlic which was always cut and pressed with the side of a knife – the mistaken call for a garlic press required me once to take cover under the table metaphorically. Another board was used for meat or onions, several were kept for bread depending on the size and shape of the loaf and various others for general purposes and in different sizes. They were stored in an open slot below the draining board. Her plate racks came from France and were chosen for their capacity to store many different-sized plates as well as saucers, soup bowls, cups and coffee mugs, providing easy access.

The kitchen worked well for her for a long time and was the scene of many hours of hard work, enriched by happy conversations and delicious meals, but it did have drawbacks. The room was damp and dark. It was jerry-built (not by her) in the 1920s, without proper damp-proofing and with little natural light, so inevitably when her old friend and tenant moved out of the basement flat, Mrs David decided to create a 'winter' kitchen in the space.

THE WINTER KITCHEN

The proposal for a winter and a summer kitchen sounded an excellent plan and I discussed it with my aunt at length. In particular she liked the idea of a larger space, more natural light (which is not hard to believe) and a 'soft' area, which was to be carpeted and an upholstered banquette installed. A small day bed was proposed for afternoon naps. The kitchen area itself would once again consist of a very simple set-up: a sink cabinet, a free-standing stove, a cupboard with sliding doors – more practical in a cramped space, she thought – and a table with semi-circular ends to make circulation easier.

Mrs David had a down-to-earth approach to the planning of a kitchen. Grand kitchens with yards of worktop were anathema to her, although I think in the 'winter' kitchen perhaps the workspace is in a little short supply. She had experienced some rather inconvenient kitchens in her time, but had learned to make do as shown in her own words by her 'Nanny's surreptitious nursery cooking. What you can cook on a stove in a passage or on a staircase landing, or over a gas ring or small open fire is fairly surprising. Granted, the will to do it, plus a spirit of enterprise and a little imagination, are necessary elements in learning to cook. You have to have a healthy appetite, too, and not worry too much over the failures or shortcomings of your kitchen and its equipment.

'During the war years in Egypt, when I ran a reference library for the British Ministry of Information, I lived in a ground floor flat located in a car park for the vehicles used by one of the secret service organisations, whose offices, in a nearby building, were known to every cab driver in Cairo as The Secret House. My cook, a Sudanese called Suliman, performed minor miracles with two Primus stoves and an oven which was little more than a tin box perched on top of them. His soufflés were never less than successful, and with the aid of a portable charcoal grill carried across the road to the Nile bank opposite (the kitchen was so small it didn't even have a window, and if he had used charcoal he'd have been asphyxiated), he produced perfectly good lamb kebabs. The rice pilaff I named after him and the recipe for it which I published in my first book in 1950, became part of quite a few people's lives at that time. When something was lacking in my kitchen, which was just about every time anyone came to dinner, Suliman would borrow it from some grander establishment. All Cairo cooks did likewise. Thus a dinner guest was quite likely to recognise his own plates, cutlery or serving dishes on my table. Nobody commented on the familiar custom.'

She went on, 'It would have been hard to beat Suliman's homemade apricot ice cream. The only drawback was the cranking of the churn, which made so much noise that it tended to bring dinner table conversations to a stand still. My Cairo kitchen, absurdly inadequate though it was, is one I remember with affection. I couldn't now contemplate cooking in such a hole in the wall, nor indeed did I then, except on rare occasions when I took it into my head to show Suliman how to cook something I had learned in France or Greece before the war, but all the same memorable food came out of that kitchen, including one year even a Christmas pudding. This pudding Suliman, too hastily briefed by me, very understandably supposed was a main course to be served after the soup, and bore it in flaming according to my instructions. Crestfallen, he took it away, but brought it back again at the appropriate moment, in undiminished style, once more drenched in rum and distinctly more alcoholic than was quite orthodox.'

All of this meant that Mrs David was relatively easily pleased and had a modest level of expectation as far as space and facilities were concerned. She thought out what her minimum standards were and had certain very definite ideas. Apart from a stove with an accurate oven, a tall sink cabinet was needed, so she did not have to 'bend double' whilst washing up. She liked a large china clay sink big enough to house at least one plastic bowl and a colander at the same time. Teak drainers were preferred; metal or granite was considered too unfriendly and would cause breakages of fine glass or china. A low table for an ice-cream maker was requested. At the time she was writing her book on ices and experimenting regularly with a wide variety of recipes.

The colour of the walls, a steel blue, was mandatory throughout most of the house and in the 'winter' kitchen too. It worked beautifully with the wood; she chose a mixture of London plane wood and English ash for the sink cabinet. It also mixed well with her favourite 'colours' – black and white. She used to wear these colours too.

The soft area of the kitchen, while not overly ambitious, perfectly suited her needs. I designed the banquette with red and black acrylic barrels as finials on the posts to link in with the inlay inserted into each vertical which were made up of alternating red and black rectangles. She requested a design that was fresh and modern, but quietly so. The handles on the sink cabinet were likewise turned from acrylic by a jeweller. This inspired her to hang her First World War poster 'Britain's bread' behind it because the colours matched the inlay. It was the only conscious effort at interior decoration I saw her make, although she was intensely interested in the design of furniture, culinary objects and in art, especially painting. When the hardback rights of her books reverted to her in the early 1980s, she republished them illustrated with hundreds of paintings, mainly historical that were connected with food; she vetoed photographs of food in her books. Much of her research for these revitalized editions was done in this room. The pendant light was a favourite, making a circle of light over the table and creating a sense of privacy and cosiness within the room.

This 'winter' kitchen, it must be remembered, was not designed for cooking family meals. It was a writer's kitchen and as such only intended for the preparation of meals for small numbers. She could always use the original upstairs 'summer' kitchen when she wanted to cook for larger numbers, although in fact she rarely went back to it.

I have quoted my aunt at length because her words are a salutary reminder that the essence of a kitchen is still the cooking and eating of food. Cooking properly is a great skill but it is also an act of love and so impacts on us in an emotional way. The smells that arise from the baking of bread or an exotically fragrant dish waiting to be eaten fills the air of the kitchen and the house with delight and anticipation, drawing the members of the household into the kitchen, making it the focal point of the house. The visible presence of fruit, vegetables, herbs, condiments and food cooking all add atmosphere, turning a collection of furniture and fittings into a living kitchen. Elizabeth David of all people had the ability to enhance our cooking skills through her writing and raise our standards so that we can enjoy food and hospitality that little bit more. A good kitchen should encourage us to cook and adapt to our own way of life.

Postscript to Elizabeth David's Dream Kitchen

By the late 1970s Mrs David's main kitchen had been featured in so many magazines and she had lived in it for so long, some 30 years, that she was well aware of its shortcomings – and keen to have a change. When Terence Conran wrote his first kitchen book and asked to photograph it, she refused. After she explained that I was designing her some new furniture for the kitchen, they came up together with the idea that she should write a piece for the book describing her 'Dream Kitchen'. She asked me to design it with her and draw up the plans. The title was a pun on the theme used in so many glossy advertisements for those highly fitted, laminated plastic kitchens that were being promoted at the time. Excerpts from her text are quoted below. The visuals have been redrawn because neither of us were quite happy with how they appeared in the book; the design is little altered but reflects better how she imagined her 'dream kitchen' to be. As usual her ideas were ahead of their time and included some down-to-earth advice, as well as new thinking. One of her major dislikes in her old kitchen was the lack of natural light and it may have been this that gave her the idea of a painter's studio with all that soft northern light.

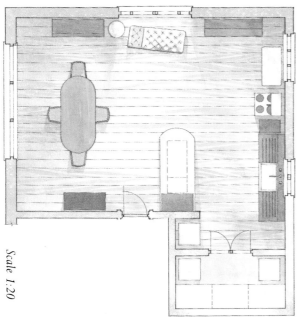

Scale 1:20

OPPOSITE
This illustration by Richard Lee is of an earlier design by me to illustrate Elizabeth David's 'dream kitchen' (for Terence Conran's first book on kitchens) which was more like a painter's studio than a conventional kitchen.

'This fantasy kitchen will be large, very light, very airy, calm and warm. There will be the minimum of paraphernalia in sight. It will start off and will remain rigorously orderly. That takes care of just a few desirable attributes my present kitchen doesn't have. Naturally there'll be, as now, a few of those implements in constant use – ladles, a sieve or two, whisks, tasting spoons – hanging by the cooker, essential knives accessible in a rack, and wooden spoons in a jar.

'The sink will be a double one, with a solid wooden draining-board on each side. It will be (in fact, is) set 3 ft 6 in (1050 mm) from the ground, about 6 in (152 mm) higher than usual. I'm tall, and I didn't want to be prematurely bent double as a result of leaning over a knee-high sink. Along the wall above the sink I envisage a continuous wooden plate rack designed to hold serving dishes as well as plates, cups and other crockery in normal use. This saves a great deal of space, and much time spent getting out and putting away. Talking of space, suspended from the ceiling would be a wooden rack or slatted shelves – such as farmhouses and even quite small cottages in parts of Wales and the Midland counties used to have for storing bread or drying out oatcakes. Here would be the parking place for papers, notebooks, magazines – all the things that usually get piled on chairs when the table has to be cleared. The table itself is, of course, crucial. It's for writing at and for meals, we well as for kitchen tasks, so it has to have comfortable leg room. This time round I'd like it to be oval, one massive piece of scrubbable wood, on a central pedestal. Like the sink, it has to be a little higher than the average.

'Outside the kitchen is my refrigerator and there it will stay. I keep it at the lowest temperature, about 40°F (4°C). I'm still amazed at the way so-called model kitchens have refrigerators next to the cooking stove.... Then, failing a separate larder – in a crammed London house that's carrying optimism a bit too far – there would be a second and fairly large refrigerator to be used for the cool storage of a varieties of commodities which benefit from a constant temperature of say 50°F (10°C).

'All the colours in the dream kitchen would be much as they are now, but fresher and cleaner – cool silver, grey-blue, aluminium, with the various browns of earthenware pots and a lot of white provided by perfectly plain china....

'When it comes to the cooker ... I'm happy enough with an ordinary four-burner gas stove. Its oven has to be a good size, though, and it has to have a drop-down door. Given the space I'd have a second, quite separate oven just for bread, and perhaps some sort of temperature-controlled cupboard for proving the dough.

'What it all amounts to is that for me ... the perfect kitchen would really be more like a painter's studio furnished with cooking equipment than anything conventionally accepted as a kitchen.'

The Extended Kitchen

Almost everyone could do with a bigger kitchen it seems, with a few lucky exceptions. It is not that most people are unhappy with what they have got or that it is a principle of science like the ever expanding universe; rather there appears to be an increasing range of uses for the kitchen in the last part of the twentieth century.

For a start, the kitchen now often has to cope with sitting room functions. I am regularly asked to make space for a sofa or 'soft' area; a desk for homework is a popular choice, also a nursery area for younger children, accompanied by a carpet as well as a toy cupboard. A table is a standard requirement but it has to be of dining room proportions. A sideboard, suitable lighting and a matching level of space commensurate with a dining room is also mandatory. Once you have incorporated food preparation functions, then you are including in the kitchen most of the purposes of the downstairs rooms of a house. It is no wonder that most kitchens are too small. Our houses were planned with kitchens to suit a much more limited set of activities.

The classic question is how to increase the size of a kitchen in the most convenient way. The answer – after nicking space from any unnecessary corridors, old pantries and lean-to sheds – is by building on a conservatory.

In the kitchen illustrated, both courses of action were adopted. A staircase was repositioned and an entrance hall removed. At the same time the integrity of the architecture was reclaimed by returning the room to nearer its original shape. However, the greatest addition of space came by building the conservatory. In a northern climate, every house needs to take advantage of all those windy autumn and spring days when the sun shines and you can bask inside its protective glass walls. The new soft kitchen functions can be so well accommodated in this way. It suddenly becomes possible to eat in natural light throughout the year – at least lunch and sometimes even breakfast and tea – and it raises the light level in the entire kitchen area. Access to light is a fundamental architectural requirement basic to human well-being.

There is another perhaps less understood gain. The occupants become better connected to the garden. Not only can you bring a little bit of the garden inside with you, but you are almost sitting outside the house inside a transparent wall of glass.

This sink cabinet has a serpentine-shaped end to ease access to the refrigerator on far left (not shown). The china clay sink is set below teak draining boards which allow water to flow into it. A granite tray surrounds the taps. Pea carvings are incised in the legs of the central island as a subtle reminder of its purpose.

OPPOSITE

A view of the kitchen from the outside door shows the central counter which is generous in size but still leaves plenty of circulation space. The Aga is enhanced by a pair of cabinets to either side and a canopy above which compensates for its traditional position in a recess.

So many houses — and kitchens, for that matter — do not connect up well with the garden. As so much effort is needed to make and maintain a garden, it seems a terrible waste not to be able to enjoy it to the maximum. If you are tucked away out of its view, it is important that when a new or extended kitchen is planned, its orientation towards the garden be taken into account, at the very least placing a window for enjoyment of a good view previously denied. If you cannot build a conservatory, then try for a terrace with a seat, pots, perhaps a raised pond or a table and chairs with access via French windows. Replanning the garden, as was carried out here, can also be used as an opportunity to enhance the connection and orientate it towards the kitchen.

In a conservatory there is the problem of dull days which can only be coped with by pulling the blinds across the ceiling. Blinds are necessary to avoid excessive glare and heat in summer, so they need to be installed at the earliest opportunity. Double glazing (even triple glazing is available now) provides excellent thermal protection, but if you still feel psychologically concerned about the cold, then a wood-burning stove with opening doors can be installed in a corner for the odd special occasion where a genuine fire makes all the difference, expelling unwanted thoughts and promoting homeliness and comfort, or it can simply be used to cut down the central heating bills.

OPPOSITE

The conservatory addition houses the table, a sofa (not visible) and a generous corner dresser. Originally there had been an old half-height window but this had been newly opened up. The whole orientation of this part of the house is thus extended into the courtyard garden, which makes possible the pleasure of eating in plenty of natural light.

LEFT

The design of the central island, although in a 'country' tradition is aimed to be light and elegant, and with light being able to travel through it a feeling of spaciousness is maintained. The ceiling was painted a dark rich red to bring the height down and create a warmer colour scheme.

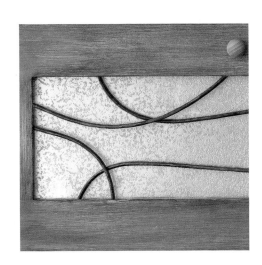

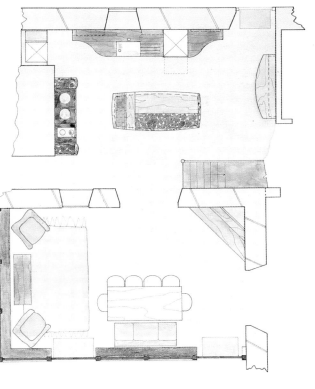

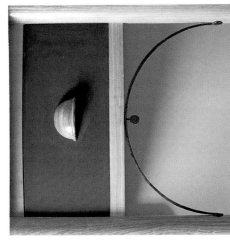

Scale 1:20

These photographs show a serpentine-shaped cupboard on the end of the sink cabinet enhanced by hieroglyphics by Felix Delmar and the client. Detail of dresser leg, and a detail of conservatory door panel with acid background and burnished forged metal rods in front.

OPPOSITE

The old staircase in the centre of the room was demolished and this new one moved to the left-hand side of the space and left open. The paintwork on the new staircase was carried out by Felix Delmar, and inspired by conversations with the client. It has become a greatly-loved feature and adds a sense of fun to the kitchen.

In this kitchen in the heart of the Cotswolds, the location and nature of the building led us to a subtle re-inventing of 'country-style' mostly through simple detailing and the use of solid English ash as the choice of wood. English cherry and painted finishes were employed to provide variety and a more relaxed atmosphere.

The kitchen is in a manor house built by prosperous farmers in the eighteenth century. It deserved a kind of quiet decorum, so the 'country-style' was controlled and not allowed to become too rough and ready as some stripped pine kitchens are intended to be. The design was aimed at achieving a balance between a hard-working country kitchen with a sense of propriety, and being comfortable enough to suit the needs of the professional family who are occupying it in the last decade of the twentieth century. I am hoping it will be suitable for the next one too, although I am sure fashions and tastes will continue to change. So it remains an open bet. However, when something is beautifully made and settles in well, it's always hard to disturb it.

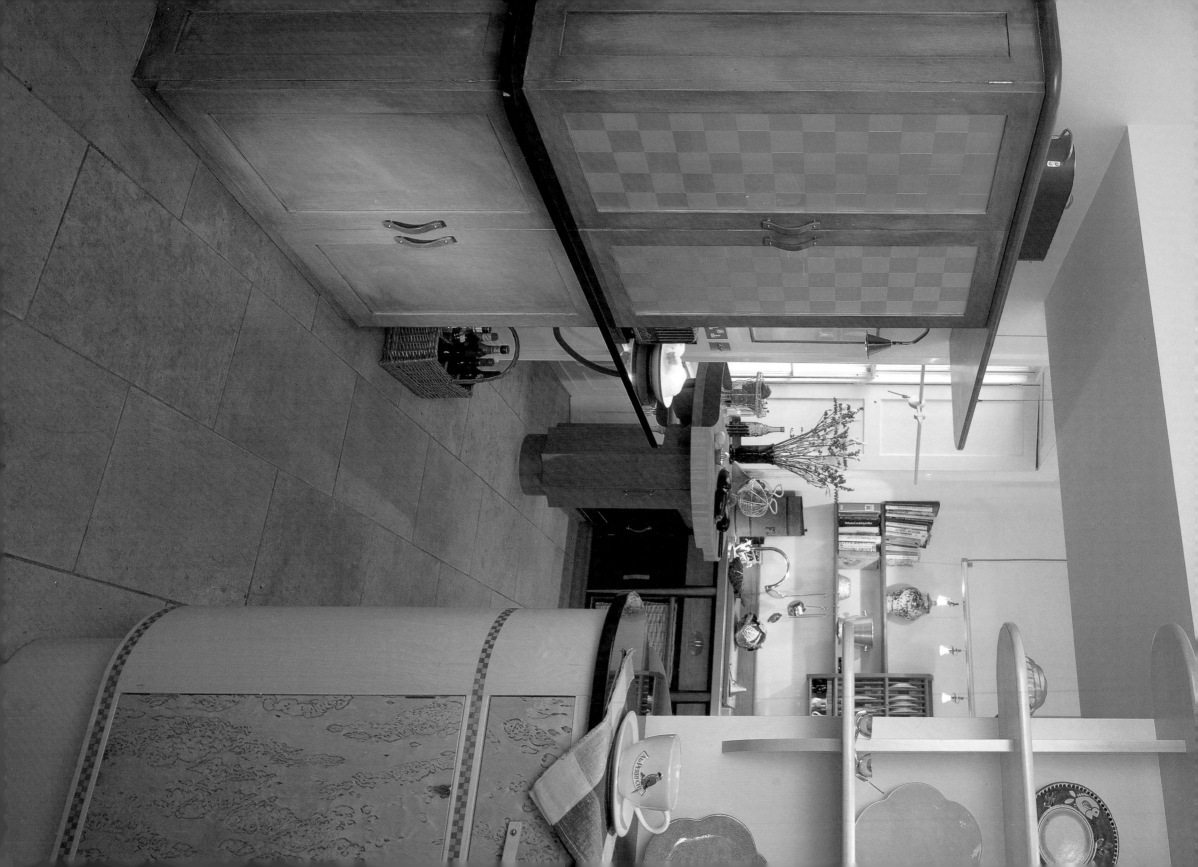

Turning Obstacles into Opportunities

What do you do when you arrive in a bare shell of a kitchen and find the client has just installed a massive 4 ft 6 in (1.38 metres) square pillar bang in the middle of the room, carefully dividing the space in two?

As you enter, a tall but narrow breakfast dresser with curved ends protruding over the edge of the pillar draws attention to itself with its rich mazur birch veneer. As you walk past and stand in the other half of the room, the cooking counter embraces it with a giant curved top. The upper part of the pillar is used for shelves and at eye-level an extractor is suspended from it, so the pillar becomes both useful and necessary.

The same sort of opportunism copes with a floor-to-ceiling recessed window. No continuous counters here, just a free-standing chopping block on a single column with the pleasure of light falling around it from the window. The top though is linked to a second sink nearby to facilitate vegetable preparation. I mention these as examples of where standard factory-made cabinets could not cope with the architecture (the window-sill is too low for a built-in unit), but individually made pieces of furniture can respond to awkward challenges.

ABOVE

The second archway shown from the cooking side of the kitchen also suggests movement, but more so with its snaky shape. It houses a vital kitchen facility often ignored — a message centre.

OPPOSITE

This view into the kitchen through the archway shows the free-standing cupboard tapering in plan so as to suggest and enhance movement between the dining and cooking area. The green paint on the cupboard by Felix Delmar was built up in thin layers and has a light watery appearance.

Scale 1:20

When it comes down to it, I think almost every kitchen has the equivalent of an awkward central pillar in some way or other. Doors in the wrong place are examples that spring to mind, not forgetting the worst problem of all – not enough space. That is where you need ingenuity more than ever. I wonder why the kitchen industry does not train its kitchen planners in the art of three-dimensional design or even some aspects of architecture as well. There are no schools for kitchen design, but plenty for motor cars, plastic products, buildings and cooking. Perhaps it would encourage too much free-thinking which is not good for sales of factory-made cabinets.

Once one is free from the shackles of a system or range of kitchen units, then opportunities abound. In this particular kitchen the ceilings are

OPPOSITE

The cooking side of the kitchen houses a giant circular work-station embracing the pillar, using one piece of granite, made by Paul Saban whose company, Stonestyle, obtains performance from masonry.

LEFT

The dresser reduces the impact of the pillar by its soft protruding edges, and turns an obstacle into a receptacle for a piece of fine furniture. Breakfast materials are kept inside, and a toaster can be used on its granite top. The wood on the panels is mazur birch and the structure is sycamore.

Floor-to-ceiling windows can be a problem for standard kitchen units, but when you have the freedom to design and make to fit each new challenge precisely what is needed, then creative skills can be called upon and anything is possible. Here this chopping block was designed to fit in the recess retaining the lower panelling and the shutters, with a continuous linked-up worktop.

OPPOSITE
The height of the ceiling gave the room an airy quality so it could absorb much darker colours on the furniture — and tall cupboards chosen by the clients. The stainless steel sink top was made in one piece to link into the chopping block.

12 ft (3.69 metres) high so there was a chance to design one tall cabinet — the red one in the photograph. Then in order to assist with circulation, the green storage cabinet under the central arch was wedge-shaped, being widest adjacent to the chopping block for use as a worktop. And the fun can really start on the colours, timber choices, detailing and finishes. This does not mean one should go crazy, merely that at some stage new ideas should be let loose and moulded into shape by a carefully balanced design strategy based on the owner's wishes.

Difficulties and constraints cause heartache at the start, but they can also force one into innovative thinking. Many architects and designers fear a blank sheet of paper or an open project, for where are the starting points? In this case it was that the room was north-facing and in the past used by servants who apparently were not in need of sunlight! Natural light and orientation of the room to the house and garden is the first issue which should be evaluated. Can it be improved? On this occasion a new window facing west gave the room a fresh lease of life and made it worth turning into a kitchen.

Planning kitchens in old properties can be a tremendous challenge and be an opportunity to turn obstacles to advantage.

The Kitchen as a Three-dimensional Painting

A painter must balance colour, shapes, texture, tone, mass, movement and light. The same applies to kitchen design in addition to the obvious practical considerations. When I was asked recently what method I use when designing, I realized that I work like an artist making a painting. I build up the idea in layers, mixing up, cross-referencing, testing and re-organizing, until finally the design has coherence. The artist's techniques are invaluable. The capacity to make the mundane comfortable as seen in Van Gogh's chair and pipe, or to make the everyday appear enticing as in Hockney's swimming pool paintings, is a reminder that it is possible to use the skills of the artist not only to give poetic qualities to a design, but also where there are widely different elements, to weave them together. Visual interest and a certain tension are needed to provide stimulation. After all a kitchen design is a visual experience.

To make a balanced design means using a mixed palette of materials and colours. As a rule of thumb that would be a minimum of two colours, often more on painted pieces of furniture. They should contrast with each other but work in harmony with the walls, choice of timber and flooring

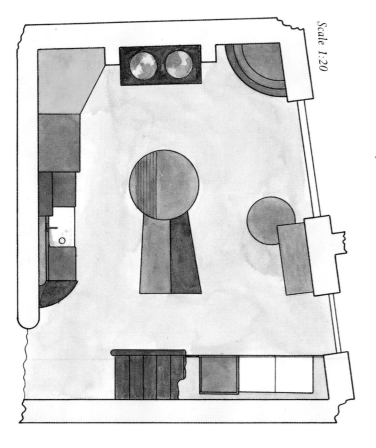

Scale 1:20

material. The inspiration for colour comes from a wide range of sources. The client's own preferences for certain colours count for a great deal; the age or period of building, and its geographical location, are important, but a major determinant is light and aspect, as well as the connection to adjacent rooms. The use of bold colours is more contemporary and the intensity of the colour will make a big impact on an emotional level. In the kitchen (shown opposite) the paint is applied in layers, so the effect on the two pieces of furniture, with the exception of the staircase cupboard, is greater, thereby heightening the enjoyment of the geometry of the grid.

The limestone floor acts as a host to the strong shapes of the furniture and has a calming effect combined with the soft off-white walls. The openness of the rectangular part of the central island helps to off-set its predominance and size, reducing its overall mass. It also helps to create an illusion of space. Furniture with open space below, such as tables and open-bottom dressers, are visually less bulky, and it is surprising how much less constricting it is to walk between two tables rather than two counters which have cupboards to the floor. One advantage is that the tables in the same space could have wider worktops without causing the visual congestion associated with what I call the corridor effect.

The central island responds to the shape of the room, with the rectangular part (see plan) following the rhomboid shape of the room. The low-level worktop is for small appliances and for parking equipment and utensils to leave the high-level worktop free. The legs are an attempt to find a new outlet for carving – an under-used craft in modern furniture.

OPPOSITE

The openness of this end of the central island creates a feeling of spaciousness throughout the entire room and lets the natural light from the French windows penetrate right up to the sink cabinet.

The client owns a vineyard in Germany and his wine label was enlarged and hand-painted on the wall at the back of the Aga cooker. The circular counter top contains an end-grain chopping block and a waste chute drawer.

The relationship between the furniture was carefully considered. The tall painted cupboards were kept simple. The cherry wood furniture was given predominance by using carving or inlay to draw the eye to specific parts. The circular drum uses inlay to enhance its circularity which is enjoyable because of its fineness. It is always a pleasure to behold a complex, well-executed piece of craftsmanship. Carving was used to lighten the appearance of legs, show off the wood grain more effectively and help to develop a contemporary language for carving; most carving is carried out for restoration work only and it is a useful tool to enrich small areas which can add character and personality to the space in a controlled way.

A good painting works on many levels. There is, as discussed, the composition with consideration of the colours, the mass, the painting techniques. But there is also the meaning of the content, the visual references, the nuances and the cultural context. In a less intense manner the same goes for a kitchen too. It is made up of images in the form of pieces of furniture, each of which carries messages about its lineage.

In being aware of what goes on under the top layer, the finished design, it is possible to see how rich the decision-making process is and how much thought and care is needed to make a great kitchen or a beautiful painting.

Intuition and Aesthetics

For a kitchen where architecture, furniture-making, interior design and ergonomics crowd into the picture with their own history, disciplines, techniques and nuances, there is a huge jumble of phenomena to sort out in order to make a design. Whilst on a practical level a plan can be tested for its workability, there is no such easy solution to making the aesthetic decisions. Many people think that these can only stem from an emotional or whimsical basis, cannot be rationally justified and so can be ignored or dismissed as being too private or personal to discuss.

It is true that the aesthetic judgements involved are partly formed by intuition but they are not to be devalued on those grounds. Intuition is based on experience combined with heightened imaginative powers, enabling one to predict one's future requirements with more perspicacity within a situation that is not yet real. It was defined in the fifteenth century as being the state where 'vision and knowledge are identical'. I believe it to be a vital creative tool and the areas where it can be made use of in kitchen design represent those parts which communicate most directly with the client and the outside world.

Intuition provides guidelines where straightforward rational knowledge or science cannot assist, and especially in answer to such personal questions as what makes you feel comfortable. Some needs, like space, warmth, light, good appliances, storage and so on, are obvious in a kitchen. But what about the other less clearly defined aspects? Colours, textures, types of wood, scale and style of the furniture are examples. The balance of architectural elements, the type of floor, the soft fabrics and the choice of accoutrements – pictures, china, equipment and other friendly clutter – show evidence of its purpose as a kitchen. A kitchen needs evidence of everyday use and its owner's enthusiasm for life. Choosing the utensils, tableware, china and cutlery is pleasurable and like any other regularly used personal belongings, these are a form of self-expression. Without the skills to make these objects for ourselves, the next best activity is to choose them. And regular use connects you to them in an intimate way and makes them 'yours'.

The cultural and visual references in the woodwork details, the shapes of the furniture – do they have echoes of other times and places? The colours – what are they reminiscent of and what are their symbolic

A table with slot for books and so on, making use of an awkward corner. Giant storage cupboard snakes along the wall, responding to the circular counter and changes wood at various stages from English cherry to sycamore. Each quadrant of the circular island had its own specialized role – preparation, washing/wet area, low-level appliance parking and the high-level servery. The inlay was made by Philip Cheshire, an inlay expert. All the timber was supplied by Milland Fine Timber, the leading supplier of ecologically harvested timber.

Scale 1:20

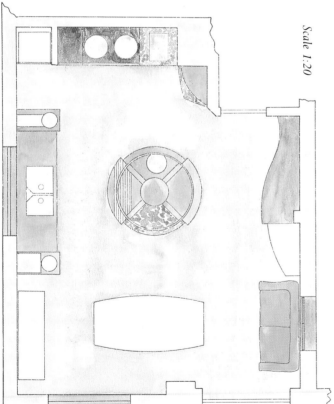

meanings? These are two examples, but all man-made objects have wider associations via personal memory or cultural history. When these are carefully understood, then the design can be both rich in meaning and achieve a kind of maturity that results in a sense of wholeness. It makes the kitchen a joy to be in and like a good work of art has an enduring quality whereby you don't get bored with it.

There is no easy escape from aesthetics. It never ceases to surprise me how much impact the last layer can make. The paint colour on the walls, the worktop materials, the floor surface, the type of finish of the timber as each one is brought in, all have a tremendous effect on the overall design. It is the relationship between these elements that gives the design its resonance, and is expressed in particular by the tension or harmony between them. Good quality materials that reflect light well, and are enjoyable to touch with all their different aspects of warmth, pattern, tone, durability, colour and origin, make a vital contribution.

OVERLEAF

The sink was designed as an architectural fitting with columns to contain it. These columns help to create an illusion of height to counteract the low ceiling height. The base of the columns contain pull-out storage on one side, waste bins on the other. The columns have storage shelves for spice jars.

88

The kitchen illustrated is in an eighteenth-century farmhouse. The furniture design makes reference to several periods. The base of the circular central island could be likened to a Victorian library drum table, although its segmented nature with different heights and with the end-grain preparation block has hints of an imaginary Rubic cube. The structure which springs from it was inspired by an umbrella and the result looks a little like Victorian railway engineering as the holes drilled for butchers' hooks remind me of cast-iron structures where the economy of material necessitates holes when the strength is not needed.

The curved cupboard which snakes along the wall in an asymmetrical fashion accommodates the shape of the circular island in its geometry. It has echoes of the work of French designer Philippe Starck, who is responsible through his love of horn shapes for reminding us in the 1980s that curves are sensual and satisfying.

The sink cabinet breaks the rule. It is not curved, but symmetrical, attached by columns to the ceiling, which turns it into an architectural fitting rather than a piece of furniture. The columns give it verticality as they sometimes can give an illusion of height to a room with a low ceiling.

The paint effects on the wainscot are carried through to the sink cabinet, reinforcing it as an architectural fitting. They have a naive American Indian flavour partly through chance, but also to reinforce its rural location and the client's interest in spiritual life. The painter, Clare Gordon, the client and I, developed the patterns in the kitchen by living with it for a time and building it up slowly until the intensity of colour and detail felt right for the room.

The whole project was done in stages. First the sink cabinet and Aga were installed. Once these were settled in (along with the clients) the central island—was designed and lastly the long curved cupboard. At each stage the design was a response to what was already there, akin to the process used in an earlier way of building before drawings were used. Decisions were made closer to each stage of fabrication and so were more immediate. Without paper and plans, building and furniture-making must have been a very different proposition. I suspect the craftsmen of the past relied not only more on tradition but also on verbal communication and intuition. A book and exhibition entitled *Architects Without Architecture* by Bernard Rudovsky in the 1960s made this point very clearly. There was little division between builder and user, and the buildings were inspired as well as practical with a strong sense of place.

Abandoning the use of plans and paper would be impractical today, but closing the gap and establishing good communication between client and designer will help to bring us closer to an earlier form of building. And a finely tuned antenna assisted by a well-developed sense of intuition helps the designer to sense the client's requirements and produce good work.

The Kitchen of the Future

When I imagine my kitchen of the future, I see a sunlit space, a large stone fireplace with an immense, slightly shabby sofa nearby, a generous-sized dining table, hand-made furniture and enough space for a desk or second table. French windows offer easy access to the garden and beyond that there are panoramas of mountains with views of the sea in the distance. I imagine myself preparing food with a glass of wine at hand while talking with my family and friends. Music offers a backdrop to the sound of warm chatter and the tantalizing combination of cooking aromas that emanate from various sources. Half-completed dishes clutter the work surfaces and casually placed bowls over-laden with fruit, nuts and other delicacies sit on the dresser offering a medley of colours, textures and ripe, sweet perfumes to remind everyone where they are when there are no cooking scents to fill the room.

My thoughts drift away to the table and I am instantly reminded that sitting down to eat with others brings with it not just the expectation and enjoyment of food — the product of the cook's efforts — but laughter, languid conversation and the company of good friends and family. It is a centre for the grittier side of life too; early morning breakfasts and late night departures, the hard work of cleaning and washing up, and the effort of despatching the children to school on cold mornings.

For me, the kitchen should raise the spirits and be a place of comfort and sociability while at the same time being physically hard wearing. Thoughts concerning the design of the kitchen start to come into focus while I mentally rebuild and play around with my dream room, moving objects, adjusting the room's central features, adding furniture and architectural elements and altering materials. Gradually, I start to formulate a sharper, clearer picture as the poetry of wishes is transformed into practical solutions to particular needs.

When planning the kitchen I first consider what someone needs to be able to cook happily in it, as this, after all, is its main function as a room. Choosing the right surfaces for food preparation is vitally important and I would select a worktop made from end-grain wood. I would have it placed near to the hob and the sink with a series of slots for knives set at the right height conveniently placed near the worktop, for easy access. My ideal stove would have at least four burners, a griddle and a wok burner, which could

Charm, atmosphere, colour and individuality: the best kitchen raises the spirits, helping to make it the focal room of a home. For me the kitchen of the future is not a technology-driven fantasy, but an expression of belief in the human need for companionship and the desire to cook for others.

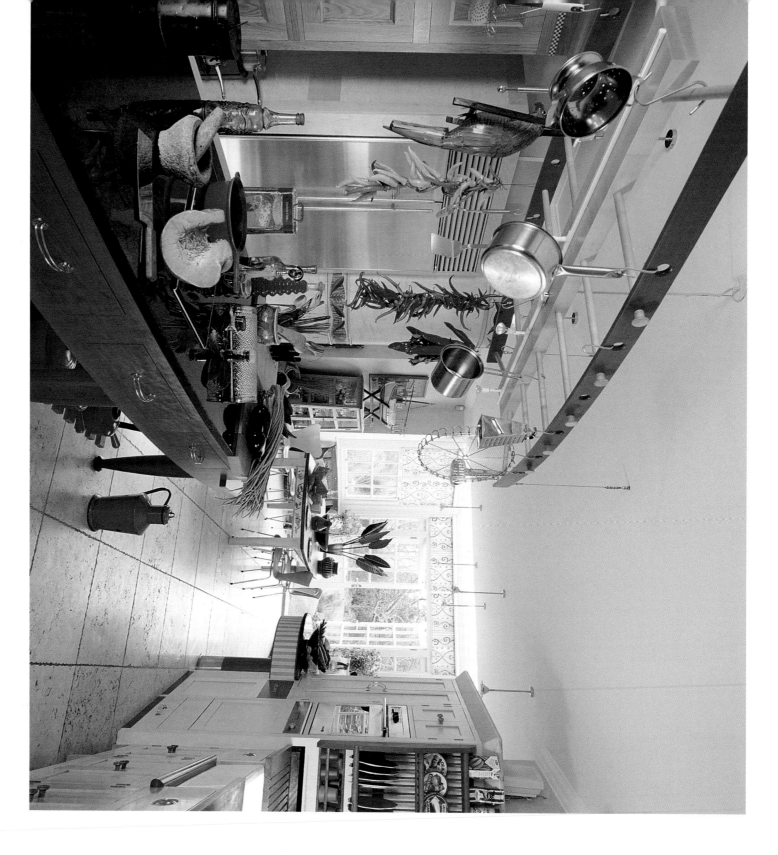

Space, generous work surfaces, natural light and materials, and a large table are some of the attributes a good kitchen needs, whether it is designed for the future or the present.

be placed at a second cooking station along with the obligatory eye level grill or broiler if space was short. I would install quiet but powerful ventilation and would create an appliance 'garage' so that weighty kitchen equipment such as food-mixers, fryers, grinders and perhaps even a proving chamber for bread-making were easy to get to. As far as ovens go I would want both a steam oven, for cooking vegetables and baking bread, and a quick-to-heat eye-level oven for conventional baking and roasting.

Set on a generous-sized, low-level countertop would be small appliances such as rice cookers, juice extractors and toasters (to stop you burning your eyebrows when you check the toast). I would want these appliances to be simple, well-made, easy-to-use and easy-to-clean and I would make sure that the worktop could also double as a children's cooking area which, if it had a granite surface, could also be used for pastry-making.

For general household administration, and an area for young children to play, a table is a must; a second table or workstation for older children to do their homework would also be convenient. I would want a large noticeboard where messages could be pinned and, alongside it, a slate tableau for shopping notes. Writing with chalk on real slate is mildly sensual. The chalk, with its sinuous and waxy texture, glides over the smooth slate making all the letters feel perfectly formed, which is why children cannot resist writing on them. I have one now and it certainly encourages me to make the effort to write up shopping notes. There is the added satisfaction of seeing one's handwriting on view, a pleasure that is rather reminiscent of playing teacher at school, a wicked delight that appeals to the child in all of us.

Another piece of furniture that can be energetically personalized, and which is also a necessary part of any good kitchen, is a hutch or dresser where food, china and the evidence and ephemera of family life can be displayed. I would like a generously-sized version with an open pot rack underneath so that I had somewhere to put my large cooking utensils.

If I achieved everything I have listed here I would consider that I had done very well. I may have missed a few desirable elements that would make up my ultimate kitchen but one thing I would not leave out is plenty of places to perch, so that those spontaneous conversations that enrich the day can just happen. It is, after all the companionship of others that really makes a kitchen live and feel like the centre of the home.

THE FUTURE ROLE OF THE KITCHEN

I am not a prophet or seer, nor have I spent time analysing social or business trends, but I can make an informed guess as to how we might live more comfortably in the future. It seems quite natural to speculate on future ways of life, especially your own, as the impact of changing your living space and the expense involved in carrying out the work involves an enormous commitment of effort, and brings major disruption to your daily life.

It is commonly accepted that the design of a house, and especially the kitchen, is guided as much by the social needs of the family as by its function as a home. The kitchen, of all the spaces in the house, has particular significance because it is more than just a room equipped for cooking. The design of the kitchen has an impact on the entire way a house is planned. For example, if the kitchen is to be a quiet room for cooking, reading and conversation the living room may be used, instead, as a TV and media room with a hi-fi system and maybe even soundproofed walls.

If the new kitchen is a sociable space then it will happily take on board some of the living room's traditional functions as a place for reading, conver-

Excellent design is about being able to successfully exploit a room's architectural features in a balanced plan. Here, a recess with a view through a porthole window into the garden makes cooking that much more pleasurable.

sation and study, leaving the sitting room ripe for TV use. But if you want soft, quiet comfort in both your living room and kitchen, then a new room is needed – a media room for television and music.

The kitchen of the future is often projected as a high-tech super-lab where the need for serious cooking has been miraculously overcome; a view that suits those from the sit-back-and-let-technology-do-it-all school. This is not a fantasy I share. First of all, I would not be confident that the food that was being served was worthy of the name and, secondly, this high-tech vision excludes people, their emotions and feelings from the familial process of cooking and eating together as a community. An added disadvantage would be the resulting de-skilling effect on everyone; children will not learn how to cook if they never have the chance to watch their parents, and adults will not develop the vocabulary of dishes needed for the enjoyment of a variety of foods, which only comes with real cooking. Being able to cook is survival instinct as well as an act of love. We would be relegated to re-heating ready-made and pre-packaged food.

This forces us to look at what we do want from our kitchens. The most influential images of the kitchen of the future are from the fifties and early sixties when miles of continuous Formica-covered work surfaces along with a stack of streamlined appliances dominated a design bred on paranoia about hygiene and a desire for cold efficiency. Neuroses about germs and the misconception that the kitchen was about feeding the family, and nothing else, resulted in kitchens that were perhaps easy to clean but lacked any element of comfort and humanity. Suddenly, all the subtlety had gone; age-old furnishing rules were discarded in return for cleanliness and speed. We really cannot let that happen again. Contemporary design, whilst admirable for its sense of cheerful modernity, needs to be careful to retain the essential element of warm domesticity.

So what is the future role of the kitchen? I believe it is to enable us to lead a civilized domestic life where we can conduct a sociable existence whilst at the same time providing hospitality for our friends and family. The kitchen of the future needs to strike a balance between efficiency and comfort. The latter is guaranteed by using traditional furnishing styles that complement our idea of home. Efficiency, in this context, means good design and cooking management so that the best can be made of the architecture of the room while at the same time ensuring it provides for all our practical needs in a form that is pleasing for us to both use and look at.

OPPOSITE

An efficient kitchen is a room that not only answers individual cooking needs but also makes everyone who uses it feel comfortable.

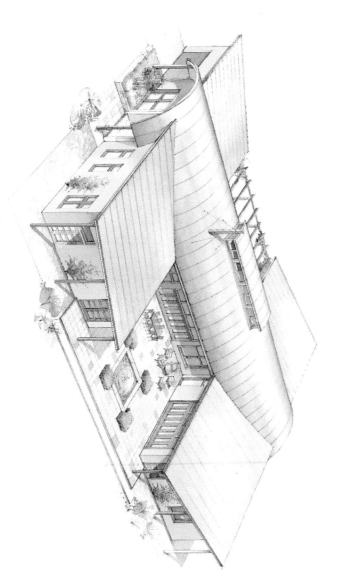

ABOVE

The kitchen is integrated into a general living area making it an ideal place for relaxation as well as for cooking.

RIGHT

The kitchen occupies the centre of the home offering both a link to other rooms in the house and a meeting place for the family. It forms a corridor through which the rest of the house must be accessed, highlighting its natural role as a focal point.

THE KITCHEN OF THE FUTURE IN THE HOUSE OF THE FUTURE

In October 1998, a well-known American appliance company called Jenn-Air asked me to make a presentation in New York about my ideas on the kitchen of the future. I decided that the presentation would focus on a house of my own design where the kitchen would be the true centre of the home.

The house has been designed so that in order to get to the other rooms you have to cross through the kitchen, effectively making it into a grand entrance hall and corridor rolled into one. It is strongly reminiscent of its historical predecessor the Great Hall, to which it is very close in concept, except that this version is better planned. It is designed to reflect the needs of contemporary life and is more focused on kitchen ergonomics having defined activity zones for eating, everyday cooking and alternative cooking

This kitchen draws strongly on the medieval Great Hall, but with a new emphasis on light and space. The dedicated work areas mean that the kitchen could parallel new manufacturing techniques where a continuous production line is abandoned in favour of focused activity cells.

In this kitchen, I identified the key cooking functions and designed individual items of furniture and dedicated work-stations to make the kitchen efficient for the cook to work in. For larger rooms, it is more comfortable to keep the activity areas compact so that large distances do not have to be covered to complete common tasks.

areas. It includes a butler's pantry for drinks, a seating circle around the fire-place and an extra table for just sitting and doing the crossword, writing shopping lists and maybe doing some light homework.

THE KITCHEN OF THE FUTURE
IN REAL LIFE

Almost all the kitchens I design are, for me at least, but I hope for my clients too, kitchens of the future. The one I have chosen to illustrate here is a particular favourite of mine and was created for a family in Wimbledon,

London. It has many special attributes: plenty of light, colour and space, and a beautiful garden outside; special and noteworthy qualities that many kitchens do not share.

Its position in the house and in relation to the other rooms is perfect. It has double doors into the living room as well as in to the dining room at the other. The kitchen is large with high ceilings so the layout is generously spaced, allowing for the inclusion of individual pieces of appropriately-scaled, free-standing furniture. The working table forms a generous preparation area. The best of modern and traditional technology has been chosen: an Aga stove, a large Belfast china-clay sink, a sophisticated air ventilation system in the cooking recess, and a Sub Zero side-by-side fridge/freezer.

However, it is the overall design sensibilities that I enjoy the most because its central influence is world music. There are references to the Caribbean in the colour and in the artwork created by Lucy Turner, bringing a wonderful freshness, originality and joy to the space.

An attractive feature of the design is that it defies you to place it in an era. There are references to many different periods and places, incorporating many subtle details and making use of a wide range of beautiful materials. To design something that lasts means evading the demands of fashion and standing firm against trends. But most of all it must connect to the building and, more importantly, to the people who live within it, making those who visit welcome by raising their spirits and producing a sense of optimism. This may sound a little ambitious but this is what we expect from great art, so why not from a sensitively and vigorously designed kitchen of the future.

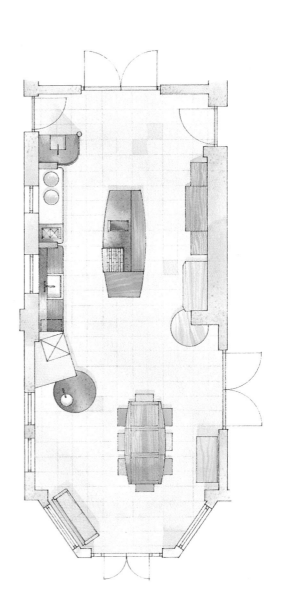

I attempted to challenge the impact made by the relatively linear shape of the room through angling the shape of the appliance cupboard next to the sink and attaching a circular table, as well as furnishing the opposite wall with freestanding pieces of tall and large-scaled furniture.

THE SMALLER KITCHEN OF THE FUTURE

Not all kitchens are large and, in response to this, Jenn-Air and *Metropolitan Home* magazine commissioned me to design a kitchen for a young, single-parent family in a New York apartment. After some light-hearted discussions with Linda O'Keefe, one of the editors, we decided to bridge the gap between the opposing trends of country style and industrial chic to create a new country-industrial style kitchen using my own design philosophy mixing built-in and free-standing furniture.

The room is triangular in shape and allows just enough space for a small central island and breakfast bar. There is a commodious court cupboard with a low-level step that acts as a platform from which high-level cupboards can be reached, as well as being a convenient perch for an impromptu chat. The cupboard also provides useful extra storage drawers. The sink run has a raised-height dishwasher. This is a welcome feature as it helps to reduce the amount of bending down needed for loading and unloading, while still allowing the countertop to be used for everyday tasks such as stacking dirty plates or putting away clean ones.

Other items include a built-in fridge, a noticeboard and friendly all-purpose dresser. The colours and materials have been chosen to give the country-industrial style a chance to claim its place in history.

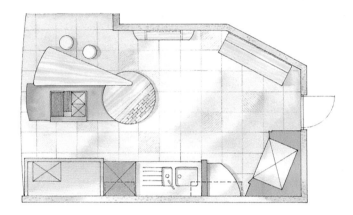

RIGHT

Vigorous planning makes the best use of this awkward space. By limiting what is included, space is left for easy movement and the enjoyment of individual pieces of furniture.

OPPOSITE

This kitchen is designed for an imaginary single-parent family living in a New York apartment. The shape of the island responds to the room so there is space for sitting at a raised breakfast bar.

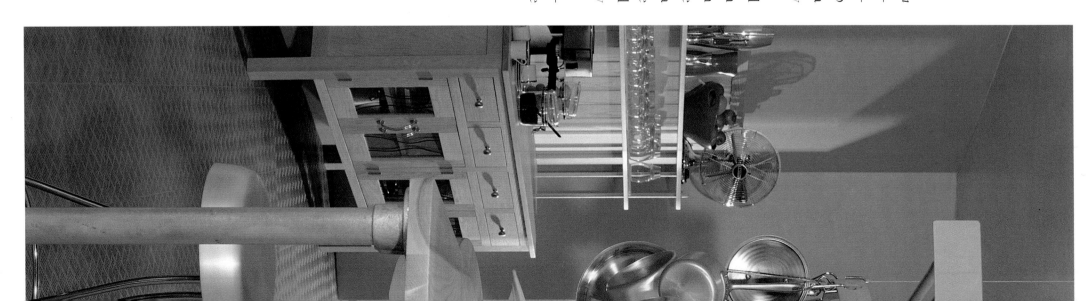

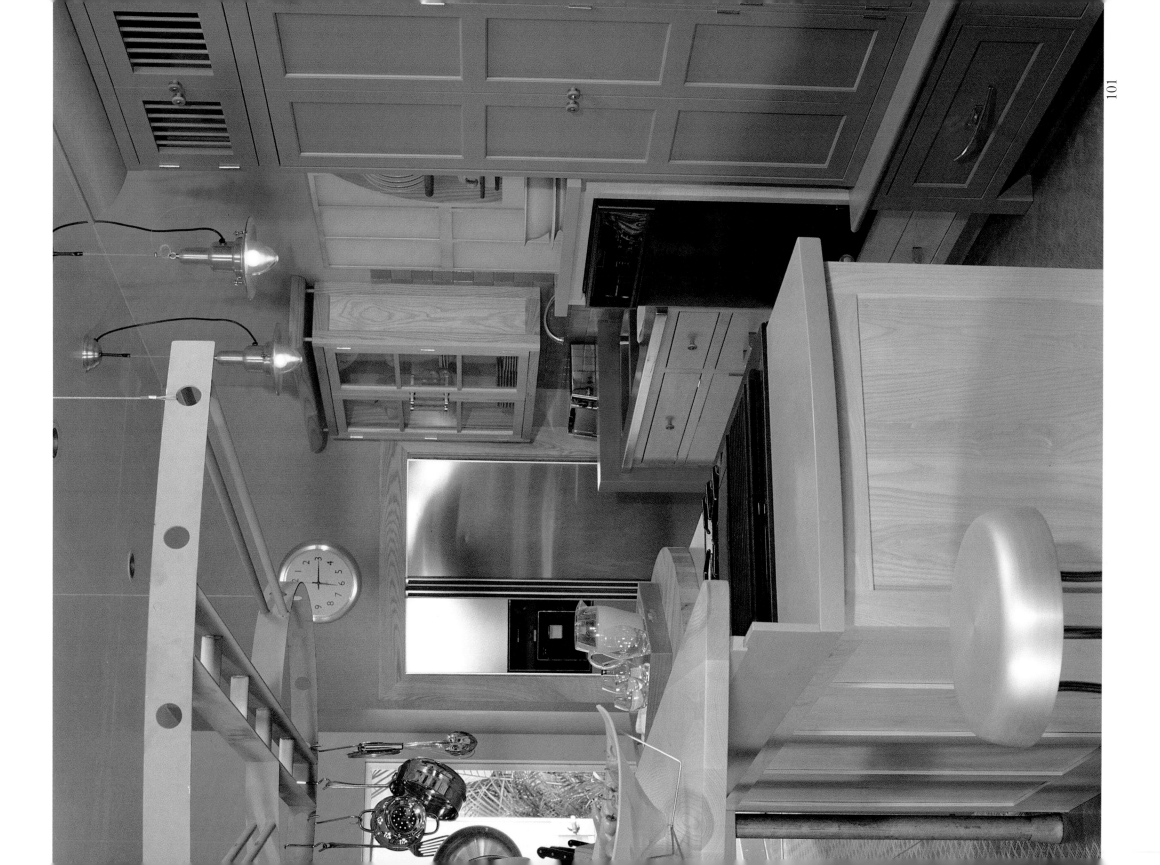

3

PRINCIPLES OF DESIGN

The Kitchen made with Furniture

In 1987 I suggested to Smallbone of Devizes that they let me develop for them the concept I had been working on over the previous ten years – the unfitted kitchen; a kitchen made with furniture. The essence of the idea was to design an individual piece of furniture to suit each function. In order to help Smallbone retail the collection, I prepared a set of guidelines for their sales staff to use.

The first one was to build as much variety as possible into the design, by alternating paint and wood finishes, by mixing two types of door panel in the same kitchen, by varying column types (applied to table, counter frames and so on) and through different roofscape choices, which are a good way of adding interest and providing a satisfying termination. The last covers any structure from the cornice upwards. There were several designs to choose from – rolling pin pediment, broken pediment, simple rail, rounded cornice, 45-degree cornice or a large roof.

Architectural features were to be preserved wherever possible. Corners, which define the architecture of a room, were to be left exposed wherever possible – at least a minimum of two. If that was not feasible, then the areas where the walls meet at the floor and ceiling should be visible. An easy way of doing this is by having a wall-mounted corner cupboard, a wall grid, open shelves or an open free-standing pot-stand (which was part of the collection) placed in the corner.

More variety comes naturally by planning a kitchen with furniture rather than continuous runs of wall-linked counters. Space around each piece of furniture can also be achieved without loss of storage, something Smallbone and I discovered by making comparative designs applied to the same kitchen, both to my surprise and pleasure. The kitchen in question happened to belong to the directors of Smallbone – Sally Wilkinson and Graham Clark. After some investigation we realized that there was a space gain through having a dedicated full-height cupboard, rather than a counter-high cupboard followed by a gap for a worktop and then only a half-depth wall cupboard above. As the most useable space for storage is between 2 ft (600 mm) and 6 ft (1.8 metres) off the floor, the gain is both welcome in terms of access and in making more efficient use of floor space. This allows the saved space to be handed over for circulation or simply to be used for creating a setting for the piece of furniture. The overall result is

that the volume of furniture is less, the architecture retains its predominance and a feeling of elegance and spaciousness can be created.

There is another great advantage of using free-standing cupboards rather than counters and upper-level cupboards. They stand vertical as opposed to horizontal, and when compared with a sink cabinet for example, the result is a well-balanced mixture of the two planes. Long built-in counters establish almost exclusively horizontal lines which take over from the architecture of the room as the dominant feature.

There was serious criticism when launched that the concept could not be applied to small rooms. If one is talking of box rooms, I defy anyone to make a sociable kitchen out of them. You'd be lucky enough to get a decent-sized sink in one of those, let alone a table and chairs. Small rooms can be accommodated but aspirations have to be scaled down and priorities established and the use of every square inch worked out. A skill a good designer or client needs to have is when to say no to additional items. A design that carries out one function efficiently is better than a compromise where either the intended flexibility of use causes it to perform several tasks inadequately or sheer lack of space makes it awkward to use.

The Unfitted Kitchen Collection was an attempt to heighten the pleasure of cooking through dedicated work areas, the use of natural materials, the careful choice of lighting and appropriate worktop heights for different activities. The space and gaps between the furniture assist in making the kitchen feel more like a living room with its dedication to comfort and sociable activities.

It was important though not to lose sight of the kitchen's primary purpose. I have long disliked the placing of a hob or stove in a row of base units because it detracts from the symbolic significance and historical roots of the hearth. This partly explains the popularity of an Aga or giant solid-fuel stove comfortably placed inside a chimney breast. The stove is the focal point of any kitchen and wherever possible this should continue. As many families want to use a variety of built-in appliances, a composite stove was designed for the collection. This enabled the cooking appliances, including an overhead canopy (containing an extractor) to be housed independently in one substantial piece of furniture, a little akin to the old ranges in Victorian kitchens. The stove could have its dignity back.

In the detailing and style of the furniture I tried to bridge the gap between old and new. Modern design often lacks detail and character. Traditional design lacks practicality and can be overbearing. Copiers of traditional furniture often adapt it poorly and because they cannot by implication add anything new, have to be looking backwards. So I attempted to design furniture with subtle but diverse references to past periods, never connecting up to any one too conspicuously. It gives the furniture an independence and charm. By including twentieth-century influences within the scope of the design an understated modernity is implied, orientating the furniture towards the future and with it a sense of optimism.

Several new types of furniture evolved. The court cupboard was inspired by the two-tiered cupboards in the Elizabethan period. The term court

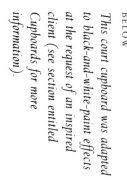

This free-standing sink cabinet with Belfast sink, teak draining boards and willow baskets, is an attempt to make washing-up more pleasurable.

Scale 1:20

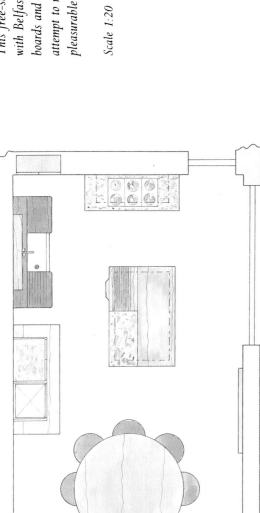

This giant court cupboard has painted inlay. It could have an additional cupboard on the top to respond to tall ceilings. The oven is installed in the corner cupboard.

cupboard was derived from the French *court* meaning short, but with two or three tiers of 'cup boards'. The court cupboard sits on a plinth that doubles as a seat for those informal moments when a visitor to the kitchen wishes to perch, and a step on which to stand for easy access to the shelves at the top of the cupboard. The step has some capacious drawers incorporated and is not too deep to stop one from reaching to the back of the main cupboard. A built-in refrigerator can be accommodated in this tier. High rooms present a problem for factory-made kitchen cabinets; most are made in only two or three heights. Without at least some tall pieces the furniture appears out of scale, overpowered by the architecture. The court cupboard with an optional add-on top cupboard makes a height of around 9 ft (2.75 metres) and befits the grandest of rooms.

Another option as far as cupboards go was the giant walk-in larder with storage shelves incorporated in the doors, borrowing from the American tradition of large practical cupboards. So instead of having to create a larder as a separate room, this was developed as an alternative. It has granite or slate shelves and willow vegetable basket-drawers.

The parlour cupboard was a response to that last bit of residual space when the main part of a kitchen has been designed. The table is usually left to last and required to be as big as possible. What is needed next to it is a

Inside the court cupboard are granite shelves and willow baskets woven into wooden frames so that the willow will last.

cupboard for breakfast material, crockery, napkins and so on. The parlour cupboard answers the need. It is narrow and wall-mounted so that a chair can be pushed back underneath it to enable one to move easily from a table that can be a little bigger through not having a floor-to-ceiling cupboard behind it.

The number of free-standing pieces of furniture in the collection made up a total of 46, which if you include the different sizes, was increased to about 170 pieces. Other variations including finishes and types of door brought the total nearer 1700. This gives an indication of the variety of choice that was possible within the collection.

For a long time before I started on this project, my ideas were being tried out on my private kitchen commissions. I designed a wide range of furniture, or adapted many new pieces of furniture for the new 'sociable' kitchen. They include a working table which is an up-graded kitchen table with a waste chute drawer; an end-grain chopping area; a granite worktop; towel rails; a storage platform and storage drawers; a series of chopping blocks with end-grain tops, some with low-level worktops; splashbacks; adjustable shelves; pull-out trays; waste chute and utensil drawers; central hanging racks in ash and stainless steel, some arched, some flat for low-ceilinged rooms; plate racks in various heights and widths; pastry dressers, one for corner use; apothecary drawers; monk's lockers for tall pans, crockery, dry and record storage; banquettes; desks; tables; chairs; wall flaps; pot stands; telephone tables and tallboys with willow baskets. With this huge armoury of individual pieces of furniture it was possible to furnish the room in the same way that other sociable rooms – the sitting room, library and bedroom – are treated which is how kitchens used to look before the factory-produced variety arrived.

This more relaxed approach results in a kitchen that is better suited to Anglo-Saxon attitudes where interiors have battered old favourites, worn-out sofa covers and Persian rugs next to brand-new furniture and inherited bric-à-brac. Life becomes a little more comfortable and the atmosphere easy-going. It can reflect the personality of the owners and avoid being over-designed. That in my opinion is a civilized kitchen.

Central Counter Rules

The central counter is without doubt the recent biggest improvement in kitchen design that has come into its own! Its recent ancestors are those centrally placed 'working' tables found in most large kitchens in England from the eighteenth century until the 1930s. Their scrubbed sycamore surfaces coped well with all types of food preparation, and in the smaller farmhouse kitchens the tables were used to eat at as well. By the 1950s with the development of factory-made built-in units we were all put to work on laminated plastic surfaces facing walls, which was anti-social and in planning terms dispersive. By placing a piece of furniture in the middle of a room, activity is drawn towards the centre. This is especially good for either large or square kitchens; the distance to be covered between the main activities is not only shortened, but the arrangement is also more sociable because one faces into the room wherever one is standing. Counters placed around the wall, particularly in a large kitchen, lead to tired feet too because one needs double the length to obtain the same amount of worktop.

Kitchen planners used to quote the famous working triangle as the basis for a good design. No more than two or three steps between each corner, please — and you had an ergonomic, easy-to-use kitchen. Apart from never finding out which three facilities were included in this triangle, I require at least 13 different facilities from my own kitchen (illustrated here) and I suspect the same applies to most well-used kitchens. I can't imagine these all being contained within the distance of three steps . . . a refrigerator, a hob, one or two ovens, a sink, a dishwasher, dry goods storage, pan storage, a table, a preparation counter, a larder or pantry, a low-level area for small appliances, a dresser for the display of fruit, vegetables and china, a servery, a plate rack and a strategically placed waste bin(s). I could easily add three or four more if a comfortable sofa, a place for the telephone, or a desk is included.

In my own kitchen the central counter is divided into four sections: an end-grain chopping block with a pull-out organic waste chute drawer; a stainless steel-lined surface with hob incorporated; a low-level area for small appliances which triples as the children's work area and eating table (with a dog-kennel, shopping basket space below); and the servery made from burr cherry. Under the hob is a second oven, a pull-out waste bin and

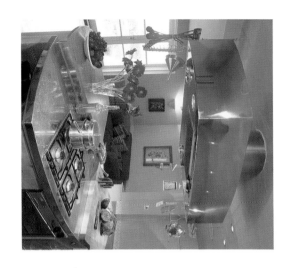

This view of my own kitchen shows the hob, extractor canopy and, in the background, the sofa. The polished-mirror, stainless-steel surface reflects natural light and limits its impact on the space. This is particularly helpful because the ceiling height is low. The room used to be a garage.

A different view of my kitchen shows the dresser, chopping board and hanging rack. Beside the windows in the background is the dining table.

an exposed shelf for the bread crock. Drawers in the plinth take large cooking utensils. The canopy above houses an extractor with its outriggers providing storage for cooking utensils and for drying out clothes in winter. Not too bad for a piece of furniture only a little more than a yard (1 metre) deep and 2 yards (2 metres) wide. Added to all this, I can chat to my family, look out of the window and see the garden while I cook and even supervise assistance when I am lucky enough to have it from the younger members of the family.

There are certain rules about central counters. Firstly, wherever possible consider making them curved, especially on the intensively used parts. This makes for easy movement around them and for transference from one side to the other. Secondly, create a sense of order by defining the activity being catered for in terms of surface material, using end-grain maple for food preparation, granite or stainless steel for cooking areas. You can alter the heights to suit each activity and assuming that food preparation is being carried out, a low-level area for all those small appliances looking for a home is vital. Thirdly, consider the design carefully. Do not over-estimate the size one activity needs as it will restrict the space available for another. Once a work area goes over a certain length, usually an arm's reach, its use diminishes. The surplus space often becomes a shelf rather than a worktop. Consider also the relationship between the activities, and how the position of other facilities, such as the refrigerator, food storage or sink affects the layout of the counter. And don't forget the space around the central counter needed for circulation and access. Finally, some kind of hanging rack or canopy is advisable both as a lighting gantry and for housing an extractor. It will give the central island an architectural presence so it no longer resembles a table.

The compactness of the island will have taken the pressure off the rest of the room, in particular to allow space for the dresser, or hutch as it is known in the United States. I have long thought that the traditional dresser one of the most civilized items of furniture. It is a necessary requirement in every kitchen for displaying the family china, kitchen utensils, fruit of the season, postcards from friends, children's drawings and a jar of pencils. Without a dresser or some equivalent piece of furniture, where else can these be kept? And without one a kitchen has little atmosphere, or evidence of its use. My aunt, Elizabeth David managed to cram three into her kitchen. All were stacked with useful objects and had their own character.

The central island makes cooking more sociable and is an efficient use of space (it has counter-space on two sides) which takes pressure off the rest of the room and allows for the inclusion of a marginal or secondary item — say, a dresser or sofa.

Scale 1:20

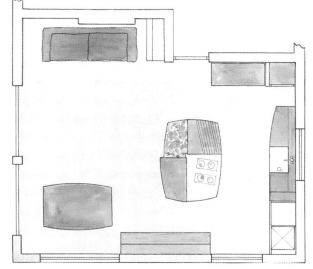

Small and Beautiful

Small is beautiful, but not too small. You cannot make a good kitchen out of a box room, but neither do you need an indoor tennis court. Over a certain size the kitchen functions become too dissipated to make use of a large space. A while ago I developed 'the arm-stretch' theory, expressed in this kitchen as a continuous circular counter where the maximum number of activities could be accommodated within the shortest walking distance. Worktop activity is defined by how far the arms stretch. Beyond that, assuming you do not wish to walk, it is appropriate to plan for another activity. Some functions, like the sink top, need draining boards on either side and require longer worktops, but at any one time only the distance between the outstretched arms is easily accessible. Over a certain length, worktops become used instead as shelf space. Miles of counter tops are unnecessary. Although you still have to walk about, by forming the counters into a circle, the different types of worktops are brought closer together and more likely to be used for their designated functions. A sense of order is engendered which results, I suspect, in enhancing efficiency in the kitchen and so making it more practical and easier to use.

Ergonomics — the study of efficiency at work — is a major part of the kitchen designer's brief. How can one make the kitchen as easy and pleasant to use as possible? The height of the worktops, the extraction of fumes, the ease of cleaning, the planning of the different facilities and their relationship to each other are important so also is the overall requirement that you should enjoy being in the kitchen. Ideally, the best room in the house should be used as the kitchen. Good natural light is a priority as well as size and aspect. Once the client has chosen the room, it's up to the designer to make it work whatever the scale.

In this extension to an old mill house the space available for the kitchen was 9ft 6in — under 3 metres — but it is possible to have four people working in the kitchen at the same time. The furniture is made of English elm and sycamore. The portholes surrounding the Aga allow natural light to travel through.

The circular nature of the kitchen allows all the main facilities to be within easy reach so bottlenecks are avoided. Every square inch is utilized, like a yacht galley. Making circular counters requires a high degree of skill and accuracy and requires the construction of jigs and templates. Even the sink had to have specialist skills to solve complex technical problems. Alan Davies of Promart, a leading expert on stainless steel, developed new tools to make it.

FAR RIGHT
This detail shows the end-grain chopping block and porthole. Every part of the kitchen has to be a pleasure to work in.

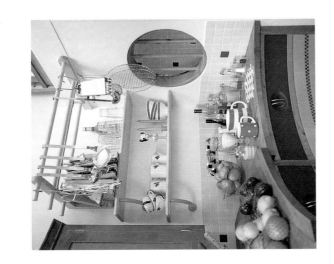

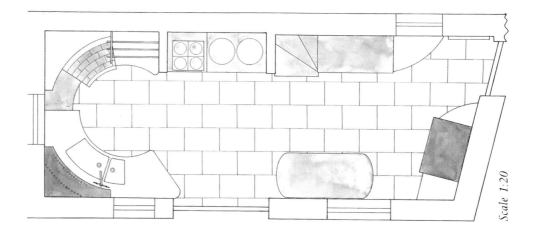

Scale 1:20

The narrow staircase provides useful storage and access to the playroom upstairs which doubles as a laundry room.

Having all the main facilities within easy reach is very helpful, but so too is having enough storage at the right height, a pleasant view, good lighting, and a plan where corridors and bottlenecks are avoided. A dishwasher raised off the floor on a plinth so that bending double to load the lower shelf becomes unnecessary is a worthwhile feature when possible. There is a trade-off because the dishwasher can no longer fit under the normal height of a worktop. Most work surfaces, sink cabinets in particular, are too low. The height should be measured from the bottom of the sink bowl as you wash up in it, not on the draining boards.

In a small space where every square inch has to be utilized, it is even more crucial to use a three-dimensional design to take advantage of every nook and cranny, rather as a galley is planned in a yacht or small boat. Likewise, the work flow should be easy as well as the general circulation throughout. A small kitchen is tested especially when it is being used by many people at once. Access to different activities and appliances must be possible at the same time. This is often hard to achieve in a small kitchen and careful thought is needed.

In this kitchen, despite its narrowness it is possible to have four people carrying out independent kitchen activities at the same time, as well as others sitting or working at the table, or even climbing the stairs. The

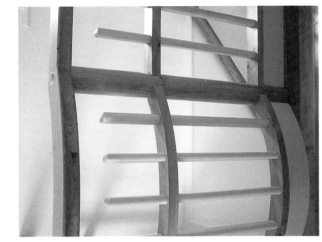

The playroom and laundry room above has toy storage facilities and space for a video, as well as for clothes. A balcony overlooks the kitchen so that children can watch the activity below.

This shows detail of the balcony rail around the staircase carefully constructed in elm and sycamore.

circular geometry is its greatest asset because it creates strong distinct pathways and circulation flow making definite patterns of movement that flow easily. Corners involve a change of direction and slow the pace of movement.

A kitchen in a small space means that your eyes are closer to the furniture, architecture and fabric of the room. The craftsmanship is therefore crucial because you are so near to it so much of the time. The same applies to quality of the materials, the finishes and the construction. The importance of minutiae like hinges, junctions of woodwork surfaces, joints and handles is exaggerated. So if you are planning a kitchen in a small space, choose the best quality of material and workmanship, put a lot of thought into it and you will be rewarded.

The enjoyment of furniture and hand-made objects stems from their material and craftsmanship. Sheer size is rarely a pleasure-giver. The way a piece of furniture is executed, the part undertaken by man, is ultimately the greatest element of the 'enjoyment' equation. Good craftsmanship, as shown by Jonathan Morriss and co-craftsmen in this kitchen and others, stimulates a response beyond the mere recognition of an efficient execution of a design. Apart from admiration for the accuracy of assembly and construction, there is a response which great craftsmanship inspires akin to the highest achievements of man: the clear perfection and mastery of a skill; sheer control of the hand, head and heart; the wonder at the complexity and focusing of concentration, time and energy to produce an object or set of objects that achieve an aura around them which demands respect, care and a quiet but continuously satisfying attention. In addition, the exquisite craftsmanship in a kitchen cabinet that one uses every day seems to make good practical sense too because it is likely to last longer.

Soft Geometry

Kitchen design starts with a good plan, the essence of which is for it to be as simple as possible with the minimum of furniture, leaving as much space as possible for circulation. Once the room has been drawn up to a scaled plan, the eye can see it in microcosm and in a detached way (by not being in the space), making clearer the do's and don'ts and the areas suitable for creative input. The natural routes between the doorways and the main kitchen activities need to be established. The furniture should try and work in sympathy with these designated pathways. People move around a kitchen a bit like water flows over a rocky river bed; they divert themselves around obstacles, make use of and fill up all available space. Human beings do not walk around corners by following a precise right angle – they take the shortest distance between two points and not necessarily in a straight line. The concept of soft geometry recognizes the principle that of the hundreds of mini-journeys that are made in the kitchen everyday, many would benefit from furniture designed using curved or soft shapes which enhance the ease of movement in the room.

The oval shape of a central island is a tremendous improvement over a rectangular one. Even though only a small amount of space is removed from the corners when you introduce a curved shape, the difference makes more impact than would appear at first glance. The other major change is the way you use the furniture itself. An oval central counter or table means you can transfer yourself from one side to the other without consciously turning a corner. It is almost as if you don't have a side or front any more, they flow together. As you get closer from an oval to a circular shape, there are no sides *per se*. This makes using the worktops much more of a pleasure.

In the kitchen illustrated here the route between the two doors suggests a straight diagonal axis between them, and it was clear that the long wall closest to them should be for storage so that the main kitchen activities could take place clear of what is effectively a corridor. A false wall was built to echo the recess opposite, which conveniently was deep enough to take a giant American-style refrigerator. I used this diagonal axis to create a deep wall cupboard set up in sympathy with the shape of the cupboards against this long wall. When the diagonal causes the cupboards to become too shallow to be worthwhile, then they become open shelves.

OPPOSITE

The central table in the kitchen doubles as the major preparation place in this writer's kitchen. The chopping block is removable by turning two wooden butterflies below the worktop so that the table can be enlarged to seat eight comfortably.

These cupboards are stepped back at an angle to make an easy pathway between the two doors into the space. Once they become too narrow for a cupboard they are replaced by shelves.

Once the stage is reached when the geometry of the plan is established as broadly workable, the design starts to take on a momentum of its own. It is perhaps a bit like giving birth to a child who turns into a difficult teenager and eventually becomes a mature adult — mirroring the design process. With the painful birth achieved — the wide spectrum of potential ideas is narrowed down into one individual persona — then progression is assured. After various stages of development the child becomes an adult and is disciplined into a coherent, well-balanced and mature individual with its own character. It is a pleasing moment when you are aware that this stage is reached. The project starts to have a life of its own. I suspect if this moment does not happen, then the project will never be a success.

In this kitchen the sink sits under the window, but leaves the corner free; in order to minimize its impact at the edges, it is curved, so that walking around it becomes easier and access to the corner drinks cupboard possible. The stove counter and central table respond to different problems. The room is not a generous enough size to have a central counter. It is only just wide enough to have a table in the middle but conversely too wide not to have something there. A crucial decision was to have a table in

The hob with open space underneath and the curved front follow the soft geometry plan. The colours were carefully chosen to make a dark semi-basement warm and sunny, but checked by a rich blue on the oven housing.

Scale 1:20

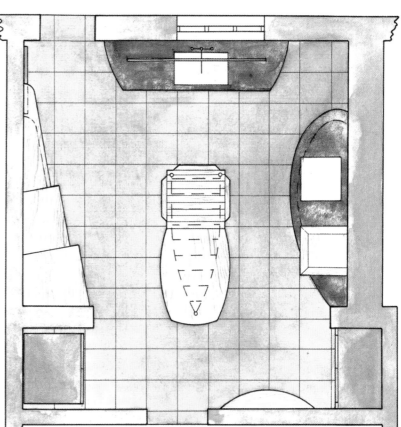

the middle, but the challenge was how to do this without making the kitchen cramped. So after much thought the centre-piece was designed as an open table with inset legs, and the stove open underneath too. As a result the table could be made reasonably wide and the kitchen does not feel too cramped at waist level. In addition, as it is lightweight, the position of the table can easily be adjusted.

The preparation worktop is a separate structure and can be removed from the table for dinner parties by twisting a turn-button concealed below. When inviting a more intimate group, those last little bits of preparation – for example, herb chopping – can be done in full view without turning your back or interrupting the flow of conversation.

The shape of the curved cooking counter allows for easy access to the oven and storage cupboard where deep pull-out trays necessitate your being able to step right back and still let another person past. One of the great pleasures of using soft geometry is that the space is made more interesting. Issues such as symmetry come up and balanced asymmetry is possible. Too much symmetry can be tiresome because of its predictability, but so can a lack of it. Balanced asymmetry for me is where you accept the principle of symmetry but apply a painter's method of putting mass, weight, colour and texture into the equation rather than just line or shape. The result is often more intriguing, more unexpected.

A riot of curves can, however, become too much of a good thing. The contrast or punctuation given by rectangular forms is necessary and useful particularly through the use of rectangular pillars. These house appliances such as refrigerators, ovens or dishwashers which are all flat-fronted and often not objects of great beauty. By being parallel to the wall, they attract less attention and can be a welcome reconnection to the architecture of the room, as well as being simpler to make.

By applying the ideas of soft geometry, maximum potential can be achieved in terms of use and aesthetics. Each kitchen has such a different architectural envelope that an individual response is vital to make the geometry of the room work. This is why an individually designed kitchen will work so much better than one composed of long straight-fronted units which respond primarily to the perimeter walls. A kitchen needs a dynamic response to a wide range of geometric demands. Soft geometry allows for this and makes for a more sociable kitchen because it can focus activities towards the centre of the room rather than the walls.

The Drawing Room and Other Thoughts

Anything goes, well almost. That is the governing proposition in a renowned book by Paul Feyerabend entitled *Against Method*. It is about how new scientific ideas are best developed. It has some interesting lessons for all of us engaged in any endeavour where fresh thinking is needed. There is no idea however absurd, he wrote, 'that is not capable of improving our knowledge. The whole history of thought is absorbed into science and is used for improving every single theory.' He went on, 'No theory ever agrees with all the facts in its domain, yet it is not always the theory that is to blame. Facts are constituted by older ideologies and a clash between facts and theories may be proof of progress.' One can substitute the word design for science and the same principle applies, only more so. New ideas often start from absurd beginnings.

Design as a discipline sits in between art and science. It has to wear two hats or many more if you sub-divide its constituent elements. The scientific part encompasses knowledge of materials, finishes, methods of construction, and the application of ergonomics. Under the artistic side comes the whole cultural input – information as far-flung as national characteristics, culinary traditions, indigenous crafts, social behaviour, a diverse range of cultural and artistic interests, styles of dress and whole local traditions of building construction. It is no less than the assessment of the whole way of life of the client, both in 'aspirational' terms and their existing patterns. The final ingredient, the imagination, plays its part as a kind of 'structural' glue. In this kitchen that inventive aspect was particularly strong.

What would be my role model for an ideal kitchen? One day lying in the bath in a rather dingy bathroom, short on both space and elegance, I asked myself this question, and the answer I came up with was the drawing room: that oasis of calmness, spaciousness and refinement. A drawing room kitchen. The idea remained dormant for a year or so until I was approached by some clients in the North of England who had bought an eighteenth-century dower house. Their children were grown-up so they did not need the capacious dining room. The adjacent kitchen was an awkward space and I suddenly thought if we could pinch the dining room and join the two together ... my 'drawing room' kitchen could be born.

This plan of the Drawing Room Kitchen allows for several activity zones as in a traditional drawing room, and each one is planned with generous amounts of space, including a grouping of furniture around the fireplace. Scale 1:20

OPPOSITE ABOVE

This centrepiece is inspired by a Victorian library drum table. It houses two chopping blocks, two cantilevered granite worktops and a cupboard below. The sink cabinet lines up with a change in ceiling level, marking the area behind as a room-within-a-room, housing a giant walk-in larder and built-in refrigerators and cupboards. The cooker is housed in an alcove as in a traditional nineteenth-century kitchen.

OPPOSITE BELOW

A double-sided banquette, one side responding to a fireplace, is designed to get over the problem of limited width in a room which was too constricted to allow for a dining table and its chairs as well as a fireplace and its circle of seating.

In this design the central piece is the preparation table, loosely modelled on a library drum table. Its classical column base makes a link to the period of the house's birth. Its circularity is appropriate because it is viewed from all sides and stands centrally. The sink cabinet demarks the change in ceiling height and hence the scale of the two rooms prior to when the new kitchen was designed. Its end columns give to it a quiet ambiguity, is it an architectural fitting or a piece of furniture? I enjoy that because it is left to the viewers to make up their own mind. Certainly it overcomes the problem of the change in height. It also creates a space behind the sink cabinet that is reminiscent of the hierarchy of a drawing room where there are clear 'circles of activity'. The main one centres around a fireplace defined by the armchairs or sofas and is followed by secondary areas, say around window seats, alcoves, a grand piano, sofa tables, bureaus or incidental groves of chairs. A drawing room suggests a space of generous proportions where it is possible to have a gracious lifestyle with several social activities being carried out simultaneously.

The same possibilities were attainable here. The fireplace provided a focal point for a 'seating' circle. Sofas were considered too bulky since space was a little tight for a grouping around a fireplace, so the idea of the space-saving, double-sided banquette was born. The clients requested a kind of Regency and naval influence to be worked into the furniture, hence the sideboard dresser against the wall.

The drawing room kitchen unfortunately never got built. The clients loved the ideas but in the end the recession hit their business too hard. A great pity. The idea lives on and the spirit of the drawing room kitchen, its atmosphere of elegance, space and fine furniture, I have taken to other projects.

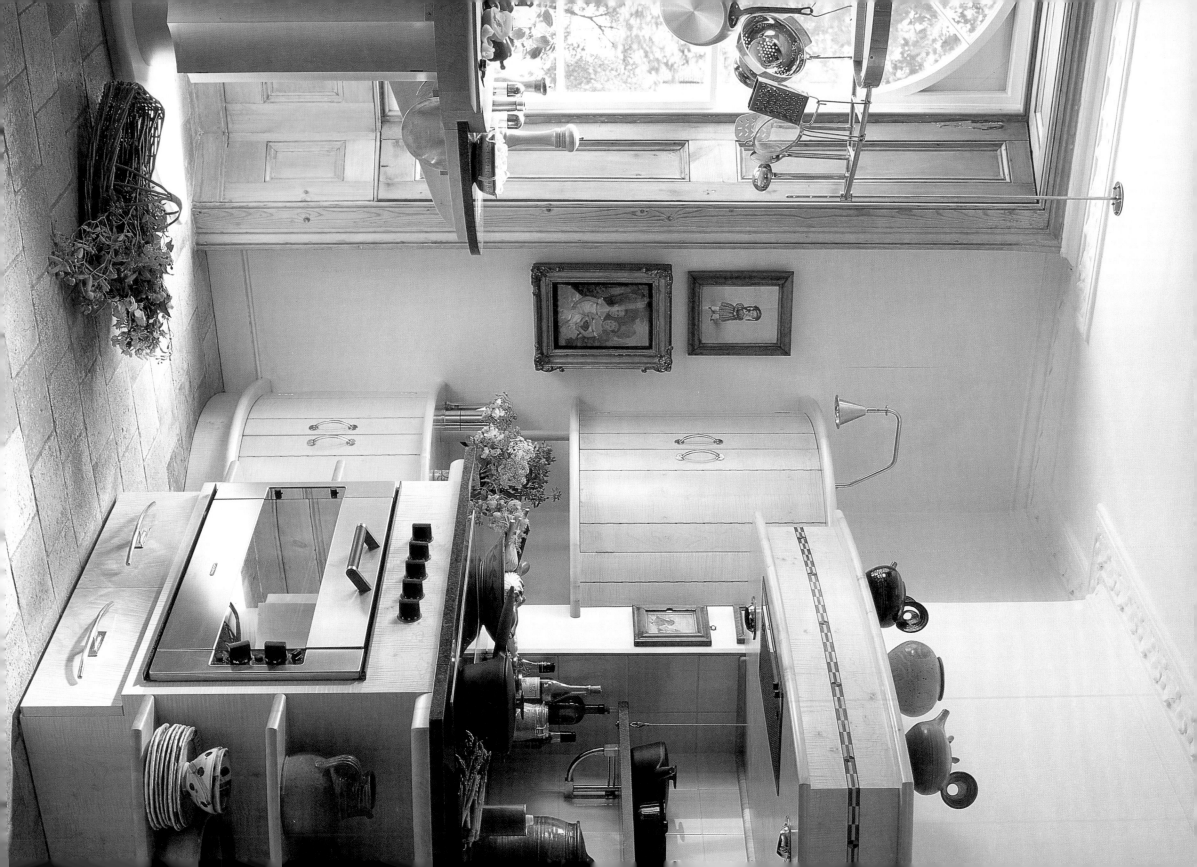

Discipline in the Design Process

The creative process is fascinating and full of mystery. Quite apart from never knowing where the ideas spring from in the first place, how are the connections made between the many different aspects of the design process? Gradually like making a jigsaw puzzle, the easier shapes – the corner and edge pieces – are assembled and provide a sketchy definition. Then a few middle clusters appear and provide a hard centre. And bit by bit the rest falls into place after a lot of experimenting on the way.

It is round about the time the hard centre is discovered that the design's personality emerges. It starts to develop its own momentum. Always an exciting moment for me, it is probably the most satisfying part in the making of a kitchen. From here on it is no longer a disparate set of inanimate thoughts, but a single living entity, no longer entirely the designer's own. Once the child is born, it has its own free will and the more mature it becomes, the more its personality and independence develop, the easier decision-making can be. It becomes possible to adopt its personality and live inside it a little. This helps one to draw the design together, enabling the addition of subtle but significant sub-themes, layers, points of interest, functional aspects, witty nuances, and links to visual historical or cultural associations.

It is possible to keep on amplifying the design. Sometimes it is necessary to take out elements, to clarify the design and make room for the new ideas. This is often hard but once done is a relief, like losing weight. The classic test is that if a component is removed from the design and goes unnoticed, it can be permanently left out. A good design has a vigour and clarity which can be clouded by overkill; a design needs constant review and stripping down where necessary.

In extreme form it is known as minimalism and is favoured by many designers. It has become a kind of cult movement, associated with Japanese aesthetics. The emphasis is on the qualities of natural materials, light and simplicity. It is a kind of purified modernism and is an extremely disciplined approach which produces a calm and ordered environment. It can also mean a dry, inhuman design devoid of the collected evidence of everyday life. So a balance needs to be struck between making a design which is both vigorous and effective, and also enjoyable, warm and capable of being inhabited in a relaxed manner.

OPPOSITE
The cupboards on either side of the stove curve into the wall breaking architectural norms. This leaves the edges of the chimney breast exposed and firmly dominant, with no long run of units boxing in the architecture.

This initial drawing proposed a simple design. There was not enough room for a centre island. The chopping block was designed to complement the tall Georgian shuttered window architecture.

The kitchen illustrated here attempts to walk on the tightrope between these polarities. They exist in most abstract inputs into the design process — old versus new, bright versus dark, rich versus simple, character versus plainness, free-standing versus built-in, curved versus straight — and are the fabric through which the design decisions are woven.

This house was built in the 1840s with distinctive early Victorian features including a curved floor-to-ceiling window and strong ceiling mouldings. There was not enough space for an island in the middle of the kitchen so the design had to be wall-based. By setting a completely independent geometry using a long curved counter, the sink cabinet made a clear contrast to the historical nature of the architecture. The design of window was suitable only for a piece of free-standing furniture in front of it, acting as a back-drop for the chopping block. Its shape was determined

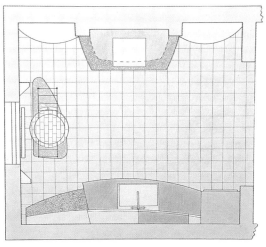

Scale 1:20

by access to the built-in counters on either side. The rack hanging above provides definition to its location as well as being useful for storing utensils and targeting electric light on to the worktop.

The cupboards on either side of the 'stove' curved into the corners at an oblique angle and break most architectural rules. This leaves the vertical lines of the walls exposed and firmly dominant … no long run of units boxing in the architecture and taking over the room here.

In terms of style there is little ornament except the inlay. Giant-sized, it is used to emphasize the long curve of the sink cabinet by running horizontally across the facade providing a logic for the changing grain direction of the veneers. Cleaning takes up time; using inlay is excellent as a source of decoration because it is part of the facade, doesn't catch dirt and is easy to clean. Inlay directs and also focuses the eye, holds its attention,

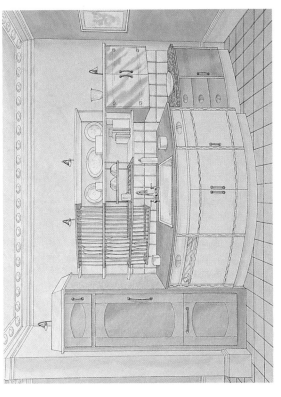

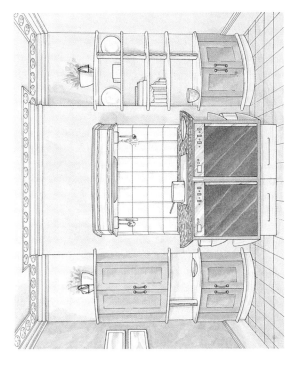

evokes admiration on account of the precision needed to make it and is satisfying on account of the sheer pleasure of repetition of a simple geometric form. I am pleased it is at last coming back into use after years of being ignored. It is an invaluable way of bringing interest and structure to facades on furniture no longer made with traditional solid timber-frame construction.

All the issues mentioned above involve judgement and skill. Every individual will have their own differing response. There are always many different solutions to the same problem, frequently equally good. In thinking them through as an exercise, re-evaluating them, it is nearly always possible to find a consensus for the most appropriate design. The art of disciplining the design, drawing out the essential aspects, rejecting the less important parts, is a skill worth developing.

ABOVE LEFT

A balance, but within asymmetry, is aimed for in this elevation showing the stove and cupboards to each side.

ABOVE RIGHT

The final design for the sink cabinet wall changed only a little from these original drawings. Principles of soft geometry were employed. The entire kitchen was made of English sycamore, the clients deciding against paint effects on any furniture.

Democratic Planning

Democracy is the means of giving every voice a say. In kitchen design terms, this means that the designer looks at the space as a canvas upon which all the parts that will go to make up the whole must be distributed in a balanced way. It is a concept that holds firm for every aspect of kitchen design, from the architecture of the room itself to the arrangement of the elements for ease of use by the cook. Using a democratic template, it is possible to balance the need for storage with the necessity for circulation and to consider these practical demands when planning the space for socializing. In essence, democratic planning is a means of ensuring that respect is shown and consideration given to all the different calls on the kitchen space. When no individual element dominates, extremes are avoided and harmony prevails.

The easiest way to tell that things have not worked out quite right is when a plan shows large areas of wall or floor space left vacant while congested areas containing a collection of elements exist nearby. Wasting space in this way is inefficient and indicates a lack of management of circulation space or acknowledgement of the scale of the furniture. There may be times when you have a big enough space to include an extra piece of furniture or an additional architectural feature to give the room an aura of magnificence, and with careful planning this can be achieved.

Democratic planning demands particular respect for furniture because each piece needs to be distributed evenly around the room so that the style, size, shape and material of each piece can make an impact. I value furniture tremendously and respect its capacity to adapt its function to suit the needs of the user and its ability to affect the atmosphere of a room. This is why I regard wall-to-wall fitted kitchens as being so destructive of ambience in a living space.

The main planning issues surrounding this kitchen in Dublin Bay, Ireland involved the need to pare down all the benefits of a big kitchen into the confines of a fairly small square room while still maintaining enough space for a good-sized table. The design offered a balance between opposing ideals. We all wanted the richness and simplicity, modernity and comfort, individuality and easy harmony associated with classic design, but were having difficulty finding a unifying idea. Our eventual starting point came from an unlikely source.

136

Using a space evenly so that you avoid overuse of some areas and underuse of others is at the heart of democratic planning. It is also a way of utilizing even the most difficult parts of the room and showing a respect for the furniture.

My clients had an unusual, but original, art collection. Having a painting to use as a colour palette and general design guide is becoming popular with our clients and on this occasion we settled on a series of three paintings by a well-known Irish artist, Pauline Bewick. We took the colour palette for the kitchen from the pictures making for an enjoyable discussion about the design of the kitchen. The materials were chosen to complement the artist's work: cherry, maple and mazur birch woods, acid-etched glass, Cornish Tordown granite and stainless steel. The colour and patina of the painted furniture, tiles and walls were designed to work conceptually as part of the paintings' domain. The green hand-painted stripes on the large cupboard harmonize with the greens used in the foliage in the paintings. The purple on the floor in the centre picture is repeated on the balustrade and the colour of the tiles is taken from the blue in the sky, and so on, making all design decisions both fast and effortless.

So in what way is this kitchen an example of democratic planning? First, the layout uses the space evenly; no areas are left under-used and the design allows you to circulate easily to all points of the room, although there are still parts that are designed for lingering in and parts that are for doing work at a desk or table. Mostly, each area has the same amount of 'heavy' use.

TOP
The details of the interiors of the cutlery drawers were tailored to meet the precise needs of the household.

ABOVE
The angled green cupboard was packed with small storage features to make as much use of the limited space as possible.

OPPOSITE PAGE & PLAN
The innate quality of the materials, woods, slate, granite and stainless steel were selected with reference to the paintings for the way they reflect light, their colour and their texture. The room was not large enough for an island, but a circular peninsula made a friendly alternative.

Each piece of furniture has a unique style, shape and colour; it has its own voice in the overall ambience of the room. The drum cupboard provides visual protection from the dining room but is humbled and brought down to earth by the microwave cabinet and its supporting drawers. The plain, linear cooking counter and sink cabinets form a geometric link to the heart of the kitchen while the circular preparation and serving drum radiates its soft geometry, making an impact on every route across the room. The flat-fronted corner cupboard above the left side of the sink is wide and slightly squat so that there is space for the paintings; the sloping green cupboard gives a hint of the Irish landscape while the table is plainly democratic with its even-sided nature. The surrounding glazed breakfast cupboard is shaped to make minimal impact and the little space that remains is spared for a cupboard. The playful mirror-backed patterns on the glass give off an air of casualness, so that the room does not appear to be trying too hard, so avoiding grand pretensions. This may sound like a minor detail but it is design awareness at this level that makes the difference between creating a kitchen that has a short life to one that will live and give pleasure for many years to come.

In democracies there is always an element of sharing and of compromise. Not everyone can have what he or she wants, even though you accept that each element must have its say and that you will have to live with decisions you dislike. In this kitchen, the shortage of space meant having to accept a smaller fridge, less worktop space, only a single sink, no dresser and a smaller table. But its diminutive size has some compensations; it is compact and cosy, and the distances between key areas of the kitchen are smaller, making working in the kitchen efficient and easy. Perhaps in this kitchen, less really is more.

Designing a kitchen may not be a political act but there is always a jostling for position between the major pieces of furniture each making a claim for prominence. So using a political analogy, the most equitable solution is to share the available space — socialist instincts but with a right-wing sense of order!

The corner devoted to the table is enhanced by a series of cupboards and drawers that create an alcove for the dining area. When sitting at the table, the cupboards make the space feel enclosed and safe. The table itself is positioned to catch the early morning sun, making it particularly pleasant at breakfast time.

4
STYLE AND DESIGN

Gothic in the kitchen, part of a long tradition of follies, shows an ironic authenticity and enjoyment of the unusual as well as evoking the mystery of the past.

The pastry dresser with gaint rolling pin has a Cornish granite surface, a pull-out drawer with milk painting on the panel and tray storage.

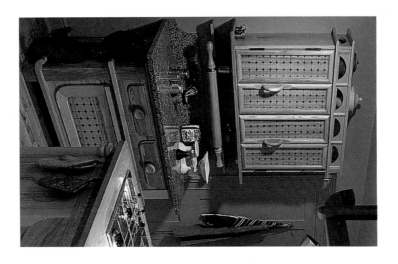

Fashion versus Continuity

How can one find a balance between innovation and continuity? The danger of concentrating too much on innovation is choosing new elements that don't go beyond the fashionable. Fashion in clothes is a useful source of self-renewal and since clothes may only have a relatively short life, it is not an absolute disaster if you become tired of them or they quickly appear dated. Furniture operates on a different timescale, and is connected with a sense of permanence. Both its physical nature and its price call for longevity. You are going to have to co-habit with it for a good many years. Your ideas, lifestyle and the demands may alter, but your furniture will not. So designing and choosing it requires careful thought and needs to take its long life into account.

One obvious way of doing this is by emphasizing and building in high quality craftsmanship. Good craftsmanship endures the test of time and continues to give pleasure even when fashions or aesthetic values change. It also ensures that the furniture will be respected and looked after. (Around 95 per cent of all Rolls-Royce motor cars ever built are still in working order, so I understand. Their quality of manufacture gives an aura that ensures they are well looked after and maintained, as well as retaining their financial value.) Any carefully made, complex piece of craftsmanship bears evidence of the skills and efforts of the maker, and the quality of materials, when combined with good design, provides a beauty and sense of completeness that creates a kind of protective field.

For a balanced design, both new ideas and old should be happily juxtaposed. The new ideas are drawn from contemporary influences, and embrace such elements as current aspects of function, choice of materials, environmental issues, new developments in technology in terms of both manufacturing and materials, and pushing the boundaries out of new aesthetic attitudes or intellectual movements such as minimalism, post-modernism, or de-constructivism.

At present there is an unprecedented climate of tolerance to the mixing and choice of styles and references. It is an exciting time to be either creating or commissioning new work. The limitations are in the over-acceptance of stereotypes such as 'country-style' and other 'labels' that limit our vision unnecessarily. By mixing metaphors and historical connections the new is developed. What has to be avoided is looking too closely

The central island has stunning views into the dining and sitting area. Furniture is in use for a long time and design needs to reflect a sense of permanence yet avoid dullness with an input from contemporary influences?

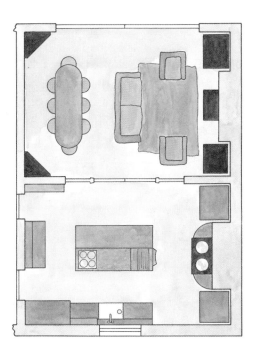

Scale 1:20

Ceiling spotlights are directed at the recessed cupboards, flanking the red Aga. Flan rings and other utensils hang from the rack above the central island.

over our shoulders to copy what others are doing. Innovation means newness and independence from what already exists. Newness in itself does not necessarily guarantee being better than traditional solutions. Sometime seeking a purely new solution can be pretentious, unnecessary or plain silly. Fashionable clothes with absurd add-ons, trivial accessories or peculiar cuts, suggest to me a short shelf life as far as user satisfaction is concerned and make one long for a more traditional design. The other side of the coin is continuity.

There are wonderful traditions in furniture-making, and in building design. Through varying them, the use of irony for example in employing mouldings but altering their scale, or by taking a traditional piece of furniture like a dresser and giving it a new specific kitchen task like pastry-making (as illustrated in this kitchen) freshness can be given to the design. Using unusual or contrasting colours on what is otherwise a traditional piece of furniture has a similar effect.

The kitchen I designed for these clients was built in 1981, and has stood the test of time well. Although twelve years or so have elapsed and my own design ideas have developed, the client tells me she is still as happy with it as when it was first installed. In planning terms it was ahead of its time – it was designed as a sitting room, dining room and food preparation area all rolled into one, and more formal than the traditional farmhouse kitchen, its antecedent. It had one major extra function: it was to be used

The kitchen is viewed from the sitting/dining area through the screen which acts as a diffuser to create a formal separation between the two spaces, while maintaining a strong connection between them.

as a small private cookery school for specialist cooking courses. Today it is still in use as such. The main requirement was a central island suitable for demonstrations and collective cooking. The planning followed traditional lines with most of the furniture free-standing. The pastry dresser and the sink cabinet are both conceived as individual pieces.

In the dining area the storage is provided by corner cupboards. The drum table, originally designed with my aunt Elizabeth David in mind, is more akin to a dining than a kitchen table. The centre-piece of the room is the fireplace and its companion, the Franklin stove. This is flanked by free-standing cupboards which house the television and stereo equipment. The screen between the two spaces creates a gentle ambiguity; is it really one large space or two separate ones? It helps to reduce the exposure of the kitchen to the 'soft' and dining areas. At one point my client's husband wanted folding doors which I nervously talked him out of. Today he's happy about this and we are the best of friends.

As far as my view of the kitchen is concerned, I almost see it as a piece of history, but am comfortable with the design. I find the red lacquer handles, fashionable at that time, something I might now want to change and perhaps I would use a little less of the olive ash which is on every piece of furniture. I'm not sure my client would agree. She likes it the way it is and briefed me clearly at the time as to the kind of kitchen she wanted. A good patron always ends up with a good job. They go hand in hand.

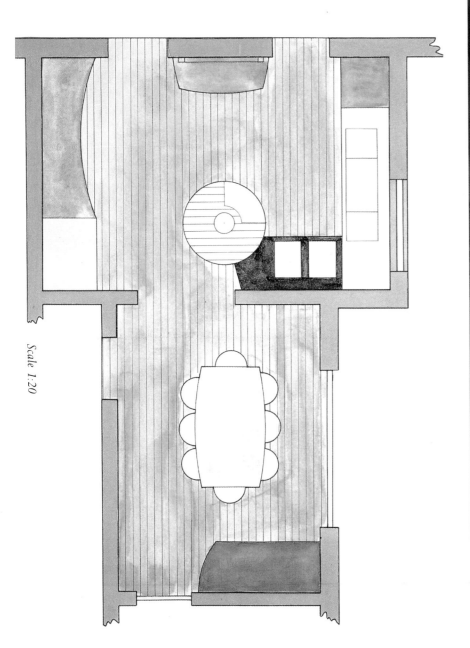

Scale 1:20

The Question of Style and Beyond

Traditional or modern, useful labels or clichés. Most kitchens are marketed under one of these descriptions, and the results are predictable. A 'traditional' kitchen is made of aged or stained wood with raised panels, doors, a scattering of suitable mouldings, a bit of fretwork, china knobs throughout and brass-trimmed appliances. If it is expensive or up-market, a few extra luxuries may be thrown in. Its 'modern' counterpart will have a consistent melamine finish, probably white, chrome handles, stainless steel appliances, plus various special features related to whichever company's products are on offer. The differences are only just perceptible.

However, I have always thought that such labels are stereotypes with little vitality left in them. It is possible to develop designs that go beyond these boundaries. For a start, the combination of the two in one piece of furniture makes for wicked good fun. A nice fat semi-traditional moulding adjacent to a stainless steel catering-style sink with dragged hand-painted cupboard doors below and giant cleat handles is my attempt in the kitchen illustrated opposite to combat these clichés. There are all sorts of other ways of going beyond them; for example, by giving expression to a fully developed idea that comes from an individual's imagination. Designers in any profession are capable of this, some better than others. Through brainstorming and the free association of ideas, new thinking is born.

There are so many cultural connections possible that share the broad umbrella of the visual arts to which the discipline of kitchen design is affiliated. The most obvious are historical periods in art, architecture, furniture and household furnishing and in different cultures. The list of wider connections is endless, but could include anything from early Egyptian sculpture – their carving techniques were simple and effective and the lines simple and dramatic – to early twentieth-century gypsy wagons where the space was planned to maximum effect and the use of timber for ornamental purposes unparalleled.

If clothes designers cross cultural divides and mix different historical periods in the same garment, then there is no reason why the thinking behind kitchens cannot be equally dynamic. Decisions about furniture and interiors are of course subject to different criteria, primarily their comparative permanence. Because you expect to live with furniture for so long, this understandably leads to a conservative tendency (same as the grand-

OPPOSITE

The client wanted a kitchen that was modern but not too glossy or overly slick. The mixture of materials was an attempt to balance traditional and modern aesthetics; the long stainless steel sink top was tempered by the rich cherry moulding below it; the blue paint finish on the sink cabinet is traditional but the drum working table is modern with clean lines. The red appliance stack is detailed with modern handles. The floor made in warm red beech off-sets the cool duck-egg blue walls.

parents, please) but it is possible to go along with this and achieve a fresh approach at the same time.

There is so much opportunity in an area the size of a kitchen where there are several pieces of furniture to accommodate, to make subtle changes of style through shape, detail, colour and material. As soon as one works out how to translate the cultural references into three dimensions, it is worth considering what is happening during this process. On a surface level it is simply a question of what a person likes, dislikes, is interested in, or has been involved with in their lives. At a deeper level it is a search for the significance of the more subtle messages that lie in all man-made objects and for what makes one feel comfortable.

In dealing with my clients or patrons I have had many long enjoyable conversations where I have been trying to formulate in my mind a picture of what their 'cultural umbrella' consists of. Each time it is so different, reminding me of the incredible individuality of each human being.

During the design process I use this information to develop the design. I don't remain a passive bystander. I add my own input because I believe that a designer is employed for the exercise of his imagination. A client appreciates being offered something a bit beyond their own imagination. A designer has to justify his or her existence too; it is his or her responsibility to question the brief to make sure it is coherent and answers the real needs of the client. Style is a difficult area because aesthetic judgements tend to be more intimate than other types of decisions but certainly where a one-off commission is concerned, it is a useful dynamic force behind the design and it is quite possible to go beyond the cliché of traditional or modern. If it is handled well, it can give the end result a quiet originality and a life of its own.

The large wall-to-wall cupboard is softened by its curved shape and broken up by the use of different panels. The tall pair on the right are mirror-backed acid-etched glass and the remainder pale English cherry.

The Modern Farmhouse Kitchen

Without doubt the farmhouse kitchen is the strongest and best loved image of a kitchen. A possible description goes like this: 'with views of rolling countryside through latticed windows, one appreciates a large inglenook fireplace, a plethora of blackened oak beams, a large open-racked dresser stuffed with china and homely ephemera, a well-worn flagstone floor, a comfortable armchair or two, a generous-sized food cupboard, a scrub-topped refectory table, and fragrant smells issuing from an Aga which announce that something wonderful is about to be served.'

It is an image replete with the signs of a happy home and a contented way of life. It is an apt description of this kitchen, sadly with the exception of a dresser stuffed with china. It may seem that the description is verging on nostalgia but the essential ingredients of it appear to me to be modern indeed. Who, with or without a family, wouldn't want a spacious comfortable kitchen, with good views, well-made furniture, evidence of continuity, and an atmosphere which is the companion to good hospitality? They are the hallmarks of a civilized existence.

The picture conjures up many wonderful images; warmth, light, comfort, continuity, evidence of the past and a rich atmosphere. In terms of lifestyle, it is the definition of a happy household, the enjoyment of cooking, a decent-sized room with a good aspect, well-designed furniture for display as well as food preparation, somewhere to relax, a big table to gather round with friends and family. Not all of these can be provided in the design, but most can be encouraged. None are dependent on the style of the kitchen furniture. I wonder if when so many people talk about a traditional farmhouse kitchen they really mean the messages behind the image rather than the style of the furniture. Can this kitchen be modern? A limed oak finish, the forged metal handles and hanging rack make it look 'old', but the philosophy with which it was planned and the handling of the detailed design is modern.

So what is modern about the design? To begin with, the orientation of the cooking activity is to the middle of the room so that the client can cook and talk to her family while doing so and not to the wall. The peninsula compacts many different activities together and allows the room to remain as free of furniture as possible. The architectural features have been retained untouched and utilized to the full. The inglenook fireplace

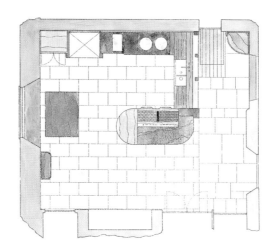

Scale 1:20

OPPOSITE
The open shelves with the traditional farmhouse china ornaments and the plate rack act as a room divider. Pans hang from hooks in the old beams above the Aga.

remains intact and the Aga provides its warmth on the wall opposite
without fighting for attention.

But most courageous decision of all, the best room in the house was
chosen for the kitchen with its view of the soft sculptured hills of the
South Downs, sacrificing its previous use as a sitting room which was
moved into a newly built extension. The table is big enough to suit a small
dinner party of eight people but still intimate enough for everyday use by
the family.

The sink cabinet with a carefully engineered two-bowl sink is deep enough to take Aga pans. With sloping wooden draining boards it is a pleasure to use, with a plate rack above that fits conveniently between two ancient undisturbable pillars! Its facade is painted so that the peninsula remains visually a separate piece of furniture and provides much needed variety of finish and colour. The limed oak finish has a function. It separates the old from the new oak, necessary because of the many beams in the ceiling and to provide a less sombre, lighter appearance on the larger pieces of furniture

Two comfortable armchairs reside by the inglenook fireplace as they did when the room was used as a sitting room. So the sociable and comfort aspect of the kitchen is well catered for – that is a modern idea too. And there is the table under the window with views of the South Downs to enrich your eyes between your roast pheasant and mulled wine.

I hope to see many more modern farmhouse kitchens, not necessarily constructed of limed oak, or in the heart of the South Downs.

The limed oak finish was given special treatment to make it textured and the inlay was featured as an architectural element rather than in its usual subdued role.

Gothic at Home

The English have a long tradition of follies. Perhaps our love of eccentricity is partly responsible. The Gothic style is at its heart. It has had as many revivals as centuries and many disguises too, secular and ecclesiastical. In the nineteenth century there was a strong connection between privacy and Gothic. The newly rich industrialists built themselves mansions or pseudo castles fortified in the Gothic style. The phrase the Englishman's house is his castle suggests the strong sense of security derived from Gothic, since that is how castles are perceived in our imagination.

During the nineteenth century there was an obsessive desire to cover walls with decorative paintings, photographs and knick-knacks of every description. This was an expression of the need to fill personal space with real or imagined experience and is part of making oneself comfortable. One reason, according to Robert Harbison in *Eccentric Spaces*, is 'the self which wants to convert its feelings for being embattled to literal fortifications'. Perhaps the regular revival of interest in Gothic is relevant today for the same reason. We want to keep the world of pollution, wars and hunger at bay. It is part of the function of the home to be a retreat or nest. Folly or comfort, for whatever reason a Gothic kitchen is chosen, it is crazy – but fun too! And surely the enjoyment of your home and the process of creating it should be pleasurable and light-hearted. If it has historical associations at the same time, it answers another need, connection to the past – a decently ancient past in the case of Gothic.

The origins go back to twelfth-century France, although the pointed arch itself can be traced back to Mesopotamia. Its use became widespread because of the superior structural strength of its vaulting. By the nineteenth century when religion dominated social values, Gothic had gained a domestic use. The medieval castle with its towers and battlements became amalgamated in the public mind with ecclesiastical Gothic developing the perfect model for a 'fantasy' style of architecture. Today a Gothic arch remains a powerful symbol, immediately evoking the past, perhaps even a slightly spooky one because of its use in historical films.

The use of Gothic is part of a search for authenticity or assumed 'historical' comfort and so is more potent than most other revivals favoured at present because of its ecclesiastical associations. There is a drawback though in the tendency, especially in the English variety, to be

159

sombre and heavy. This can be remedied by using colour, lightweight mouldings, a mixture of horizontal and vertical planes, and the element of surprise. The unexpected will always give amusement, but if it is carried out with a skill so that some aspect provides a quality of permanence, for example through complex or testing craftsmanship, then it goes beyond the ephemeral and will endure.

As it happens, my first kitchen was designed in Gothic and although every piece of furniture was made from a different style of Gothic, there was a clear family resemblance. It was an exercise in artifice. However in the kitchen illustrated here, the existing architecture of the room was so clearly to be respected that Gothic seemed the natural starting point. As the idea was to use the majority of the space as a sitting room and library, so the plan evolved of a galley kitchen in which two towers house appliances such as a tall refrigerator and dishwasher on the inside and the dreaded television on the library side. Inside the kitchen every square inch has been accounted for, making maximum use of the restricted but convenient compactness of the kitchen area.

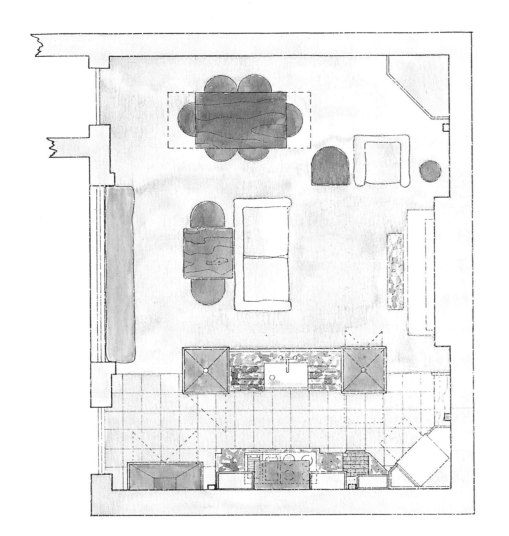

Scale 1:20

PREVIOUS PAGES
Every square inch of this kitchen is planned and fully utilized. The use of Gothic is part of the need to fill personal space with real or imagined experience and is part of making oneself comfortable. The tall cupboards contain a dishwasher (with television facing the sitting area) and on the far side is a full-height refrigerator.

TOP
This tall storage cupboard with an oversized cornice incorporates a domestic cupboard in the side panels.

ABOVE
Solid pewter handles were specially turned and the willow baskets were designed with wooden frames.

OPPOSITE
The corner cupboard oven was designed to maximize the use of the corner because the ovens address the centre of space.

It remains a peculiar feature of Gothic that almost every domestic style of architecture has at some time been 'Gothicized'. In that first kitchen of mine, known as 'Sam's' kitchen, French ecclesiastical Gothic rubbed shoulders with eighteenth-century Chinoiserie Gothic, nineteenth-century Gothic, early Georgian Gothic and Islamic tracery which goes back to its use in Syria at the time of the Crusades. Sam's kitchen was installed in 1976 at one of the darkest periods of English domestic design. The only kitchens available were made of melamine or Formica in factory-made units. They were so dull, unimaginative and uniform I wanted to send a message out that there was an alternative. The prevailing Modern Movement ethos at the time forbade ornament, historical connections of any sort and evidence of any hand-made traditional craft skills. Gothic seemed a perfect sort of defiance and act of rebellion against the then current restrictive practices. Whatever else, it certainly inspired a great deal of discussion both at dinner parties in the kitchen and newspaper columns outside it.

Thankfully today the prevailing intellectual climate is less dogmatic and more tolerant to a wide range of different styles. References to past periods are acceptable and restoration is no longer a dirty word. In some ways Gothic, the language of eccentricity for many years, is now that of good taste. Gothic has finally come home and has been made 'comfortable' to live with.

The Gothic theme was handled sensitively and the client had a clear idea of how to interpret it to make it pleasurable and comfortable to live with.

A Kitchen for the City

By the late 1980s country-style kitchens had become so popular that no other seemed possible. Many people, including myself, were sickened at this lack of choice and paucity of imagination of the bigger English and American kitchen manufacturers. So I began to develop ideas that could form the basis of a kitchen suitable for and inspired by the city.

Images of country life provide nourishment for us and are reflected in the styling of many of the products we buy. Rural life has an appeal as a place of refuge and a liberation from the pressures of a hectic and crowded urban existence. It is a major component of most people's idea of a 'good' life. The underlying images are both real and necessary, but I wanted an answer to the question, is there an alternative set of images behind urban life? And could they form a back-cloth to a kitchen design series for a big manufacturer? My thoughts turned to past periods when urban life was glorified and there appeared to be many examples.

Modern urban architecture may have failed us in recent times, especially Le Corbusier with his 'machine for living in' ideas, but that is recent history. Further back, successful examples flood into my mind. The Italian city states – Venice, Siena, Pisa, Florence – or further back in ancient times, cities such as Rome, Pompeii and Athens are all good examples of places where an urban existence would have been highly civilized. Their ways of life and cultural activities have been hugely influential both in historical terms and for those living at the time. Cities must have then been looked upon as desirable places to live. It is only recently that many cities have become bloated in size and blighted through the pollution and ugliness of their industrial areas. Smaller cities and towns are often exempt from such associations and are still good places to live. In terms of architectural design, many great British architects made their name by working in the urban landscape. Robert Adam, Inigo Jones, John Nash and Lutyens, to name a few, all evolved large-scale building schemes that had a genuine urban character.

Contemporaneous eighteenth-century furniture-makers managed to do equally well; Hepplewhite, Sheraton and Chippendale all produced designs that evoked sophisticated, cultured, non-rural images. Historically influenced to some extent, the furniture still demonstrated many new ideas, mixing references, materials, finishes and shapes that emphasized

OPPOSITE

Sheraton, Chippendale and Hepplewhite produced furniture designs that evoked sophisticated non-rural images. Their furniture was refined, elegant and decidedly non-rustic. This kitchen in Little Venice, London, is my attempt at establishing a contemporary design for kitchens suitable for the city.

ABOVE

The planning of the kitchen was simple but the detailing was refined with emphasis on the quality and mix of materials, handles and use of inlay. The timber chosen was sycamore, a finely grained wood which reflects light in an interesting way and is enhanced by irregular patches of beautiful, rippled grain pattern.

OPPOSITE

The appliance stack shows the light reflecting rippled sycamore patterns.

elegance and finesse. These qualities speak to me of an urban rather than rural character. Exotic veneers, geometric inlay, ormolu accessories, fine carvings, slim legs, delicate mouldings, fine turnings, neat metal handles, intricate marquetry are all visible in their furniture — surely some of these qualities could be incorporated in a range of kitchen furniture suitable for urban life in the twentieth century? There are many good examples of furniture-makers and designers who have done so already in this century. Eileen Gray in France and all those associated with Art Deco, Rietveld in the Netherlands, Thonet in Austria, Gustav Stickley in the United States, Mackintosh in Scotland, and many others have produced wonderful work.

When I first suggested the idea of a contemporary urban-inspired kitchen series to the furniture company Smallbone, they were not too convinced, but once I had presented drawings to their directors, Sally Wilkinson and Peter Sheppard, their enthusiasm grew. They launched it on to the market in 1991 and it has become known as the inlay range because inlay plays a major part in the visual language. The use of sycamore, previously an under-used wood and considered wrongly as a weed tree, gave the design elegance and simplicity. The wood has a cool subtle grain and takes on the colour of pale honey, associated often with the birch used in Biedermeier furniture.

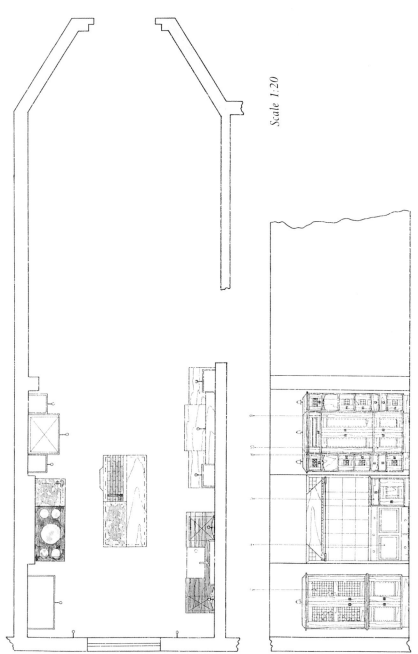

Scale 1:20

This is a classic Biedermeier secretaire bookcase. Biedermeier furniture, originating from the Austro-Hungarian Empire and Germany from the early nineteenth century to the 1870s was the first serious or 'grand' furniture to be domestic in its aspirations and designed to be independent of its architectural setting. Mostly made in pale local fruitwoods, with carefully chosen veneers, it used elements borrowed from neo-classical architecture — such as capitals and entablatures — as well as local influences.

RIGHT AND OPPOSITE

The giant dresser has side cupboards showing the acid-etched glass pattern.

The kitchen also unintentionally shares some other similarities of attitude with Biedermeier — emphasis on veneered surfaces, use of simple lines, distinct metal handles, use of inlay and no nonsense detailing. It also has, I hope, in common with Biedermeier, a sense of quiet fun, including unexpected elements such as cupboards linked into a series of intriguing repetitive small lockers, funny hats on storage pillars, doors with miniature glass windows, arches with stainless steel rails sandwiched by sycamore keystones and the mixture of wood, metal and acid-etched glass in new configurations. The whole design aims to be restrained and easy to live with, and relaxed enough to be suitable for old or new houses. The furniture should fit happily into a cold northern climate house or the warmth of a Mediterranean villa. Most important of all, it has a distinct twentieth-century urban quality of quiet good comfort and makes no reference to any country-style aesthetic whatsoever.

I find it interesting to speculate as to what would have come about had a client commissioned a kitchen from the furniture-makers of the Biedermeier period (1815-1848). Kitchens were not then places where good quality furniture was considered appropriate. Houses or apartments in Vienna at the height of the Biedermeier period were small and the interior spaces were designed for intimate family life. I feel sure that a decent kitchen would have been welcomed and encouraged a more democratic sharing of making family meals. Biedermeier furniture was a conscious reaction against the pompous and grand scale of French Empire where each piece was consigned to a special position and the furniture assumed an architectural role, according to Angus Wilkie in *Biedermeier*.

Pale woods, simple detailing and quiet consistency were aimed for in this sycamore kitchen designed for a London house, from the first contemporary range that I designed for Smallbone.

Biedermeier furniture was perhaps the first serious furniture to be made that was partly domestic in its aspirations and interiors show the emphasis placed on comfort and thrift compared with the period prior to 1815. The new furniture lacked the gilded ornaments of previous styles and even its arrangement in the drawing rooms of the time was more casual, comfortable and with greater attempt at being functional, especially the cupboards and chairs. The end results could have made some wonderful kitchens and terrific heirlooms – if only they had been made!

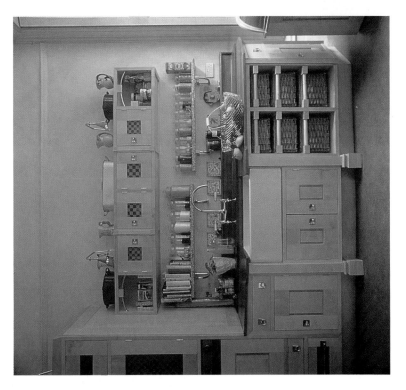

ABOVE LEFT

A minimal palette and materials were employed in this sink cabinet with storage lockers above.

ABOVE RIGHT

The chopping block, low-level worktop and hanging rack above exemplify the maximum use of space without resorting to cupboards.

It is interesting that today our kitchens replace the drawing rooms of previous times as the room in the house which requires the greatest financial investment in furniture and fittings. In many ways the kitchen is the new drawing room, for we entertain in it and are happy to be judged by our choice of furniture and the decor in general. Like all household objects we choose them because they make us feel comfortable and they are an expression of a wider cultural interest. It seems clear that the kitchen has now assumed a new level of importance in the hierarchy of images that make up our idea of house or home.

In city life a retreat from the noise and bustle of the streets is a vital requirement for one's sanity. In the newly important kitchen still at the heart of the home, a contemporary design which is a restful and comfortable space goes a long way in my opinion to making a civilized urban existence possible — and looks towards the future rather than the past. It could also give a boost to our rather tired and dissatisfied attitudes towards the city if at least we felt comfortable about the validity and underlying civilized nature of city life. Leaving behind images of the countryside in their rural setting could be quite refreshing too.

5

PLANNING YOUR KITCHEN

Starting Out

This chapter gives advice on designing your kitchen. It offers a more practical guide to creating your own dream kitchen. What follows is a series of helpful starting points.

Mixing the potential with the prosaic

What is needed initially is to be both playful and pragmatic, mixing the 'what if' scenario with the 'what is'. Try to be as flexible as possible in your thinking so that you avoid getting bogged down in details and unworkable ideas. You could start by compiling two lists; one setting out your practical needs, the other, a wish list. The former will probably be based on your ergonomic needs and the latter on the bigger picture, in particular the architecture of the room and the way the kitchen will fit into your lifestyle. Both can help you to focus on the bigger picture and the detail, helping you to answer questions such as whether the kitchen will be used as your only dining room and whether you will be able to make space for a sofa? You will want to make the most of natural light in the room, and maybe you will want to incorporate a dresser or separate barbecuing area or even an appliance garage into your plans. Only you know what you want in your kitchen, so try to consider all your wants and needs.

The nature of the room

Begin by looking at the sort of room you have before deciding what kind of function it can handle. What does it suggest or preclude? For example, where does the natural light come from and what takes priority, the eating table or the sink? The table does not want to be right next to a door or in a thoroughfare, but preferably in an alcove or position that feels secure. The room may benefit from being opened up but this might mean that the increased size would take the main preparation area too far from the sociable area of the room. Alternatively, you might prefer the cooking facilities to be out of view from the room. High ceilings and grand Victorian plaster furniture and other fittings.

PREVIOUS PAGE
The idiosyncrasies of this attic
room in a New York Show-house
allowed me to separate the
kitchen into sociable and working
areas to maintain a sense of
intimacy.

LEFT
The shape of the wall cabinet
mirrors that of the main
preparation drum amply
reflecting my principles of soft
geometry.

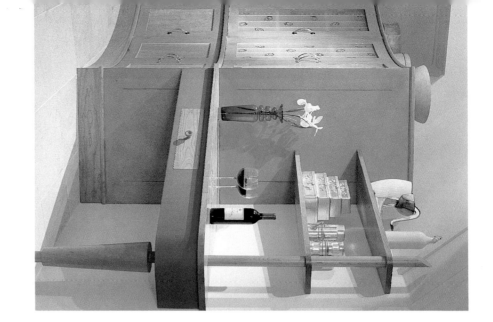

Curved furniture in a kitchen eases people through the space without threatening them with sharp corners or uncomfortable body movements. Here, a large cupboard and a casual table gently arch away from the island in the centre of the room to make the most of the space available.

mouldings call for generously-sized and vigorously-shaped furniture that will not be overawed by its surroundings. This means minimizing the numbers of pieces and making sure they are of an appropriate scale.

Key kitchen work decisions

How do you like to cook? How much work surface do you need? What appliances appeal, what size of fridge do you want and how many sinks would you like? Think carefully about distance and where you place key appliances; you may not want to be running across a vast kitchen between the hob and the fridge when you are in the middle of making béchamel sauce (see the chapter on the Small Kitchen). Think about whether you want the dishwasher to be kept on the periphery of the main cooking zone and whether there is space for a raised height dishwasher with a china storage cupboard immediately adjacent.

Dedicated work areas

When planning your workspace, make sure you create a sense of order. Plan as efficiently as possible and use the concept of dedicated work areas to guide you. This means minimizing countertop space to what people will use rather than ending up with more than you need. Too much countertop space in one area may spoil another by using up valuable space that would be better used for a separate activity elsewhere. Another disadvantage may be that key elements are distributed over the entire room instead of being close by. This could mean you would end up running from one end of the kitchen to the other. Varying the materials used for the worktops and their height will also help to define a particular area's function. Different materials bring varying technical advantages; granite is resistant to heat and water while end-grain wood is less susceptible to knife marks.

Social areas in a working kitchen

I always try to make sure that at least two of the main culinary activities, cooking and eating, can be carried out facing into the centre of the room and an island is the perfect solution to this problem. To create a central island you need a room of at least 13 ft in width (4 metres) and 15 ft (4.6 metres) if you want counters running around the walls as well.

If you do not have the space for a central island, you could create a circular peninsula instead. I have a general dislike of peninsulas as I think

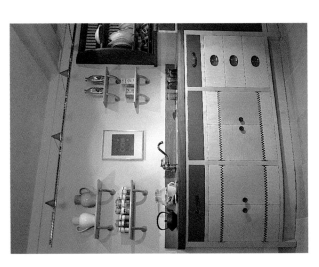

they create obstacles in crucial areas and prevent easy movement around the room (see the pictures in the Democratic Planning chapter). But the best examples, if done well, have soft curves and make a good second choice.

Architectural review

When looking at your room, think of your kitchen as a space first and as a kitchen second. Then imagine ways of improving it in your head before getting involved in practicalities and focusing on specific features.

Consider whether the envelope of your room can be extended and whether windows and doors can be altered with advantage? Are there any irritating architectural elements like unnecessary or badly positioned doors that waste space or block the circulation of the room.

Allocating space for different activities and areas

The average size of room chosen as a kitchen has increased in the last decade but often the extra space is not used for culinary activity but to make room for social activities. Eating areas take up a lot of space. The sofa too, takes a fair chunk of floor space because it needs an area in front of it for loungers to stretch their legs. A kitchen desk and a dresser are popular in a sociable kitchen, so the pressure on the remaining space is intense. The need for a tightly integrated cooking area remains, and if anything, is increased because the whole kitchen is now exposed to the public gaze; the kitchen is, after all, now on view to every visitor.

Soft geometry

The linear nature of long rooms would, in most conventionally planned kitchens, result in long, continuous counters that would form unforgiving and relentless straight lines and result in space being inefficiently used. Alternatively, a softer, more sympathetic geometry shows an understanding of the way people use and walk around rooms. By minimizing hard corners, forming counters so that they appear to wrap themselves around the body and by accepting natural paths between work areas and doors, it is possible to make using the kitchen easier and more of a pleasure. It also brings a sense of sculpture to the furniture design and if executed sensitively, allows the shape of the architecture to be enhanced.

Thinking about children

Kitchens that young children are going to spend a lot of time in need to be well thought out to avoid hazards, provide facilities for play and create areas where children can do their own cooking. The most immediate requirement is to avoid hard corners, especially on central islands and the corners of countertops. Children need low-level areas where they can cook. These low-level areas have the added benefit of doubling as parking areas for small kitchen appliances. Use granite or any other hard wearing material for rolling out pastry and make sure there is a power point nearby so that the food processor can be used for making cake mixes and so that the children can help with other appropriate tasks. Low heat glass on ovens located below the counter is a good idea and make sure that the temperature of the hot water is controlled so that there are no scalds on small hands when they undertake the job of washing the dishes.

Lighting

It is crucial for the comfort of everyone who spends time in a room to get the lighting right. It is even more important in kitchens, for both practical and aesthetic reasons, as the kitchen is used as a creative space as well as for relaxing and eating. Different areas of the kitchen require different types and intensities of light. Countertops need task lights above the work surface set halfway between the outer edge and back of the work surface so that you do not work in your own shadow.

The table needs its own separate lighting environment, with control over the brightness provided by a light-dimming system. You may also need specific lighting to suit the architecture of the room, for example to light alcoves, paintings, fireplaces, and pieces of furniture or dark areas. General lighting may also be needed, especially if there is a lack of natural light or if the room is large. The key to manipulating artificial light in your kitchen is to ensure that you have control over separate elements through separate lighting circuits. Avoid bland light and aim at installing specific or task-focused lighting. Leave some areas unlit to create contrast and shadows; otherwise you will destroy the atmosphere and sense of drama that good lighting creates.

There are new, computer-controlled systems available that make mastery of light in your kitchen easier. The brightness of sets of lights on different circuits can be pre-set to 'scenes' of your own choosing so that when you switch on the lights different modes can be selected. The scenes could include full light for cooking, dim light for romantic dining or early morning 'wake up' lighting for dark winter days. The recent advances in lighting include a huge range of low-voltage lights that are discreet in size and can be fitted in small areas such as under cupboards or in shallow-depth joists in the ceiling. This facilitates enormously flexible and imaginative lighting scenarios for every situation. (For further detail see my book *Kitchen*.)

Built-in versus unfitted

I have a preference for using free-standing furniture whenever possible. Loosely furnished space makes for a more relaxed atmosphere giving furniture breathing space that makes it look better. It also makes a room feel more spacious and airy and less crammed with stuff; hence the phrase unfitted. There are some areas of a room, such as tight corners and alcoves, when free-standing furniture is not suitable. Try to find a balance between the two and aim to keep the built-in furniture at the centre of the cooking area and the less fitted on the fringes of the room.

Furniture values

One of the reasons I enjoy planning kitchens is that I love furniture, and in most kitchens there is an opportunity to place well-designed, original and functional pieces in the right place. It is also a chance to invent new pieces too or just reinvent familiar ones. When you walk into an antiques shop, the first thing you notice is that every piece of furniture is different. These days, with most furniture produced to suit factory production techniques, there is an inevitable blandness and lack of personality in most items. We have a chance to address this gap by commissioning one-off pieces for our own kitchens.

Storage

Large storage facilities are best deployed on the perimeter of the main working zone where full height, floor-standing cupboards can be placed. This is the most efficient ratio of floor to storage volume. Too much countertop and you will limit this option. (This is why it's best not to over-do countertop areas). The use of wall-mounted cupboards above a run of counters not only reduces visibility and access, but also is wasteful of storage space, as these cupboards are not usually particularly deep.

Smaller cupboards can be installed in any available nook and cranny, throughout the rest of the kitchen. Pull-outs are useful to make access to

This giant cupboard provides a wide variety of storage options. The central area is a larder for dry goods while smaller side cupboards provide room for pans and space for a microwave. The scale of a piece of furniture is an important aspect of kitchen design.

sub-counter cupboards easier while bottle racks, spice racks and lid holders can be placed on the backs of cabinet doors. Shallow-depth cupboards in places where a full-depth one is impossible are underrated. We sometimes place them on the wall where you might normally only have room to hang a painting. I treat them as a '6 inch deep' painting, dividing the façade up into a grid. I would then ask an artist to make a painting across the whole surface. The grid creates smaller units of storage, so providing an opportunity for placing groups of items like spices, dried herbs, jams and condiments and dried fruits in their own individual cupboards.

One useful fallback for storage is hanging racks. I would normally use them as a lighting gantry but they are useful for small utensils too or big pots and pans if you hang them higher up. Evidence of kitchen life seems appropriate although it can be overdone. I recall with amusement my aunt, Elizabeth David saying, 'not for me the riots of hanging ironmongery – pseuds' corner I'm afraid'.

A *few points on measurement*

The employment of ergonomics, the study of the working needs of the human body, is a vital element for good design. I have identified some pivotal rules that should be observed for your kitchen to be comfortable to work in.

- Counter heights should hover somewhere around your flexed elbow.
- The sink should, at the highest, be around 2 in (50 mm) below your flexed elbow.
- The height of the food preparation surface should be 3–4 in (25–50 mm) lower than your flexed elbow.
- The cooking area should be 4–5 in (50–60mm) lower than your flexed elbow.
- A low-level area is appropriate for the use of small appliances. You need a surface of table height or a little higher, around 30–34 in (750 mm–850 mm) from the floor.
- The amount of space between counters and door openings varies but a minimum of 35 in (800 mm) is needed and around 4 ft (1.2 metres) is ideal.
- Space is needed around a dishwasher for loading and unloading and an oven door of around 2 ft (600 mm).
- Dishwashers should be raised 14 in (300 mm) from the floor so the lower shelf can be reached without bending down.

CASE STUDY: THE URBAN FAMILY KITCHEN

In this plan, two rooms have been knocked together to make a large kitchen that is lit by both eastern and western light. It is a good study in how to cope with the difficulties presented by a long room.

In this kitchen, the chimney-breasts are the dominant architectural feature. The problem we had was that they take up a lot of floor space and, although the house is an historic building, we discussed removing at least

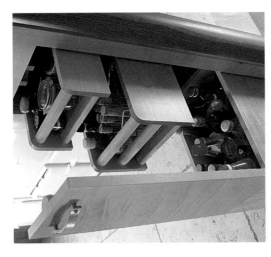

These tiered drawers provide excellent storage in small enough sections to make finding things easy. The design makes good use of a narrow space that might otherwise have been wasted.

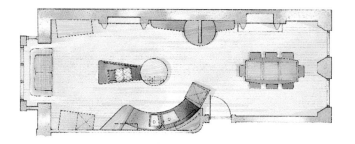

ABOVE
Long rooms can turn into
unsociable corridors when fitted
units keep people's faces turned
to the walls. Placing a sofa at
one end of the room and a dining
table at the other helps make the
room feel less elongated. The
curved sink cabinet and drum
cupboard separate the kitchen
from the eating area.

RIGHT & OPPOSITE
The large, curved cupboard
softens the opening between the
dining room and kitchen. Light
bounces across the surface in a
pleasurable way, making it a
useful feature in both rooms.

one of them before realizing that they broke up the long walls and gave focus to the dining area furniture.

The owners of this kitchen decided that although their lifestyle did not include the need for a formal dining room, they still wanted a traditional dining table. The problem was solved with an extendible table that is covered with a heavy-duty, rubber-backed cloth so that the children can use it for painting and drawing when it is not being used as a dining table. The clients' wish list included a giant multi-purpose cupboard and, by using a circular drum cupboard, we were able to soften the rather rigid opening between the two rooms. This device also avoids the problem of having too many cabinets over-crowding the recesses either side of the chimney-breast, which would spoil the symmetry of the dining room fireplace. It also softens the access point between the two rooms.

The raised-height dishwasher helps to provide privacy between the dining table and cooking areas and the curved shape of the sink cabinet helps reduce the corridor effect of the room. The hand-painted striped green pattern gives a softer, more casual effect and breaks up the determined geometry of the curved sink cabinet.

In this kitchen, we planned an island from the start. Using counter tops would have meant that anyone working in the kitchen would have been covering uncomfortable distances to reach all the key utilities in the kitchen. We minimized the distance between the cooking, washing up and food preparation areas to the shortest possible, about 6 ft (1.8 metres), while at the same time avoiding cramping the space by putting them too close together.

Closing off the old hall door formed a dedicated cooking area, which made it possible to have a longer sink cabinet and to cut down on unnecessary circulation from the front hall, so reducing crowding the key cooking and washing areas. In this unusually long kitchen, the location of a sunny alcove at the far end of the room just asked to be filled with a sofa or set of café chairs and table. We ended up by creating two sociable areas in the kitchen, sandwiching the cooking activities in the centre.

The success of this design is in its use of soft curves. The sink cabinet wraps around the central island and creates a sense of movement that allows the two to connect. The shape of the kitchen also produces shorter distances between key areas as well as a making it easier to move around the far side of the room. By making a clear choice against using the long, party walls as a basis for all kitchen activities, the central island becomes a possibility. This in turn results in a more compact and efficient kitchen that is easier for cooking and living in.

OVERLEAF

This kitchen is extended beyond the working circle to include a cosy living area with a table and sofa. The opening makes good use of the light so that the room feels airy and spacious.

183

KEY DESIGN POINTS

Below are some key points that will help you successfully design your own kitchen.

• Use free-standing furniture wherever appropriate, and leave breathing space around each piece, preferably a minimum of 12 in (300 mm). Learn to enjoy the individuality of furniture and take pleasure in the ambience that their different designs create.

• Think of furnishing the kitchen like any other room by including antiques and odd or witty pieces; try to find room for a couch and definitely aim to include a dresser or hutch and maybe a rug in the non-cooking area.

• Introduce at least two different styles of design in the door panels. Variety is the key. Use three or more different woods, lots of different door and drawer handles, and a range of shapes, colours and materials.

• Use ergonomics ruthlessly; keep distances between vital activities to a controlled minimum. Make sure your countertop height is correct and provide a low-level area both as a place for children to cook and as a parking area for small appliances.

• Balance is vital. Think of kitchen design as an art, like making a painting. All the key aspects need to work together in tension and harmony.

• Have fun and try to avoid standardizing elements. Think 'freedom' not 'conformity' and try to include some of your own personality into the room. Also try to extend your imagination. Educate and test yourself a little and take a few risks.

• Retain architectural features, like fireplaces, and respect the style of the house when deciding how to treat the fixed elements like floors and windows.

• The corners of a room define the space. Leave at least two corners visible or free of objects, especially at the point where the floor meets the ceiling.

• Avoid using mounted cupboards on every wall. Restrict yourself to individual units wherever possible. Long rows of cupboards restrict visual access to countertops and they look boring. They also offer a poor ratio of wall space used to storage space supplied.

• Try replacing wall-mounted cupboards with floor-standing, full-height cupboards. Go for cupboards with a narrow depth so that you have a clear view of the contents making small items easily visible.

• Create perching points in the kitchen so visitors have somewhere to sit for a short while. This encourages people to visit the kitchen for brief chats while someone is cooking.

6

IDEAS IN DETAIL

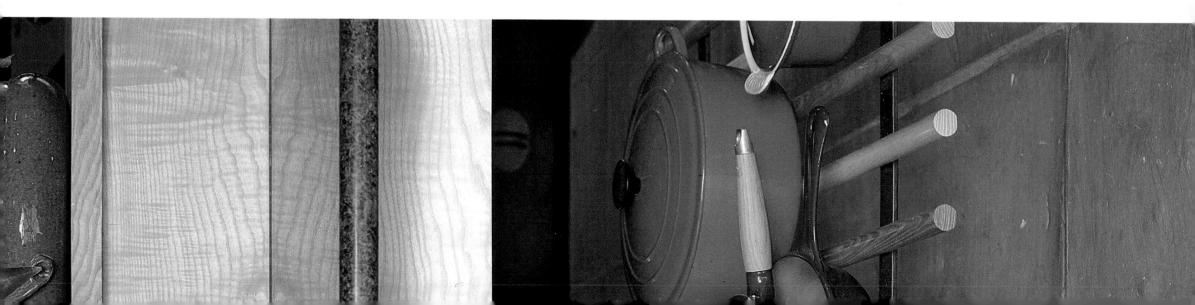

INLAY

Inlay provides an ideal source of decoration in a kitchen. It helps to focus the eye, emphasize lines either horizontal or vertical and enhance the randomness of wood by contrast to its crisp geometry; it is relatively inexpensive to make and easy to clean. Inlay creates structural order in the absence of traditional panel-frame construction. What could be more ideal. Every kitchen could use some. A few guidelines though may be helpful. Consider using it rather like icing on a cake: too much and the impact is lessened, but too little or the wrong scale or size and the result is weak or pointless.

The size of inlay needs to alter according to the job it is doing. For use vertically it is operating as a column and so a larger size is appropriate, perhaps with a directional pattern as opposed to a static one such as simple squares.

Inlay was first used in the sixteenth century primarily for denoting the panel or surface to be decorated either with carving or marquetry, the latter in particular after veneered furniture was introduced in the reign of Charles II. Giant inlay patterns were also used to provide an alternative to

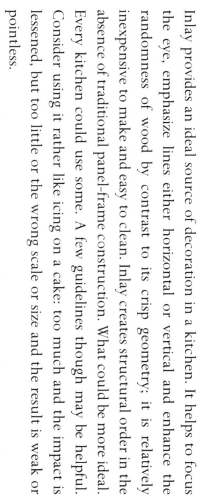

ABOVE

Inlay made in walnut and boxwood is being used here to act as a column. This innovative technique gives interest and structure to furniture or architectural fittings.

RIGHT

Inlay is used here in a traditional way as banding. It is made in ecologically harvested timbers supplied by Milland Fine Timber. The dots are hard to make and a special tool needed to be developed. The inlay was made in Amboyna and Celtis.

PREVIOUS PAGES

Suspended rack below a kitchen table, in English ash and burnished hand-forged metal.

carving, perhaps on grounds of cost, on court cupboards, in horizontal elements in preference to mouldings.

It seems there was a gap in its use until the eighteenth century when Chippendale and others used it between 1765 and 1790 in fine elegant sections to suit the delicate neo-classical furniture of the time. After this time marquetry and inlay were to a large extent superseded by painting.

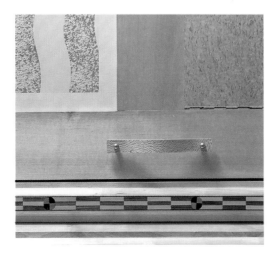

I find the early medieval inlay more relevant because the furniture was bolder and the inlay more interesting for being enlarged to the point where its complexity is enjoyable at a distance as well as close up. The scale of a kitchen – which is in essence a room set rather than a series of single pieces of furniture – calls for a more purposeful and vigorous type of decoration.

Inlay has been in the doldrums since the 1920s when it came back into use for a short period, in particular to give definition and structure to veneered surfaces in the absence of traditional panel and frame construction. Endless sheets of veneered boards with the grain going in one direction lose the pleasurable structure of solid timber panelling with the evidence of joints, grain direction and colour changes inherent in traditional furniture-making methods. Inlay allows you to have a purpose or a defined area for different grain directions and to highlight changes in plane. The sheer satisfying quality of the repetition of a complex geometric pattern – one of the fundamental principles behind decoration – should not go unmentioned, nor its execution by the craftsmen who make it. Admiration of skilled work is an undoubted pleasure.

FAR LEFT

Rectangular sections of inlay show directional movement and are excellent for use in columns. Here walnut and sycamore are mixed into an English birch frame and mazur birch lower panel. The inlay down its side is a miniaturized version of its giant neighbour.

LEFT

This inlay banding is mixed into a circular cupboard door to emphasize its geometry (see Small and Beautiful section).

ABOVE

This giant herringbone pattern is used as a column made from oak, walnut and sycamore.

PAINT AND PATTERN

The impact of the final surface finish in furniture and interiors can never be exaggerated. It is greater than it deserves to be. Using colour through paint not only provides a flexible and powerful way of determining the atmosphere and mood of the room, but also allows a closer involvement with the more emotional aspects of a client's needs.

The irregularity and variations visible in a painted surface introduce a kind of waywardness and human element into a designed space that can provide a sense of relief and contrast, working against the sometimes intimidating quality of the perfect edge and flawless surface. Hand-made objects often have more richness than mass-produced, machine-made ones because of the evidence of the human hand. The kitchen is a space that needs poetic qualities as well as pragmatic ones. The beauty of preparing food, eating and conversation is real, although for much of the time it may be forgotten through haste or routine, so recognition of this in the design and decoration seems appropriate.

Choosing colours is one of the most difficult jobs a designer can do, especially if resolving differences of opinion between a husband and wife. Our experiences and associations of colour are so deep-rooted that they are often hard either to understand or explain. Subjection to any kind of scientific rule book or definable, objective criteria is impossible. It seems choosing colours is an emotional issue.

There are, however, a few guidelines that are helpful at a pragmatic level. Firstly, analyse the varying natural light levels at different parts of the room. Secondly, be aware of whether you are contrasting or working with other elements in the design. Both techniques work well for different reasons. Too much wood in a kitchen can be tiresome and light-absorbing. Colour can counteract this; its intensity affects our emotional response and there are ways of controlling this. For example, by applying several thinly pigmented coats of paint, the colour can be strong but not intense, whereas strongly pigmented colour increases emotional intensity. In large areas a subdued colour may be easier to live with. The alternative is to confine the rich intense colour to small areas such as bands or panels. This applies to using pattern as well which can also help to subdue large panels of intense colour.

Another major contribution of paint effects is their use in highlighting various parts of the design, by applying a skilled artist's eye and hand to special panels or bands and friezes. This tradition goes back a long way, was revived by the arts and crafts movement and is an excellent way of bringing artists' work into everyday life. I particularly like the compromise where the use of repetition and small panels produce simpler forms and strong shapes that provide resonance of a wide cultural context, with hints

Although some of these designs for painted bands by Lucy Turner are certainly less complex than others, the work shown here was intended to be jewel-like in its detail, colour and fine execution, yet bold enough to create an impression immediately upon entering a room. It is worth considering both the satisfaction of close encounter and the view from a distance in decorative detail if the work is to be successful and interesting for years to come.

Panels or bands on furniture are often a good place to incorporate brilliant colours that might be too strong if painted on larger areas, particularly walls.

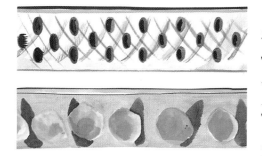

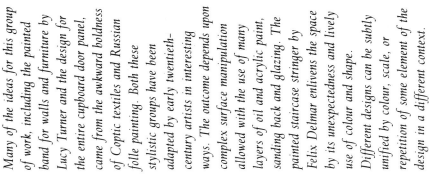

Many of the ideas for this group of work, including the painted band for walls and furniture by Lucy Turner and the design for the entire cupboard door panel, came from the awkward boldness of Coptic textiles and Russian folk painting. Both these stylistic groups have been adapted by early twentieth-century artists in interesting ways. The outcome depends upon complex surface manipulation allowed with the use of many layers of oil and acrylic paint, sanding back and glazing. The painted staircase stringer by Felix Delmar enlivens the space by its unexpectedness and lively use of colour and shape.

Different designs can be subtly unified by colour, scale, or repetition of some element of the design in a different context.

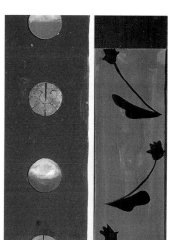

of abstract connections to other times and places. Over the years craftsmen have adapted ornament and pattern from symbolic or religious sources for easy repetition by simplifying them for their particular medium. For example, Persian carpets have complex and rich symbols. The patterns are derived from religious traditions to give meaning, shared messages and identification with their work. Lucy Turner and Felix Delmar, the artists I have worked with, are doing the same in a contemporary context, but with a wider range of references since our cultural life extends over an enormous area with diverse inputs. By re-interpreting these, adding their own imagination and painting skills, they bring a resonance that imparts subtle abstract qualities to the kitchen.

PLATE RACKS

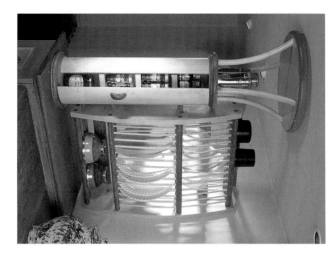

Plate racks are great inventions. Mistakenly many people think of them purely for draining plates and so on, when their function is as much to do with easy access and storage. Having designed around ten different versions, I am beginning to get to grips with their problems as well as advantages.

Initially I started off by holding the plates in position with dowels at the back and location slots at the front. This allows the rack to be used for

thick pottery plates and soup plates. A little more care is required when storing the plates because you have to fit the plate into the front slot.

A second type has vertical dowels at both the front and the back. This makes 'slamming' in the plates easier, but soup plates, pottery plates or plates with deep rims or flanges will be too thick, unless the gap between the dowels is widened to such an extent that you need an inordinately wide plate rack which does not store too many plates. A third type with dowels on both the back and floor is hard to make satisfactorily and I am currently experimenting with it. There are a number of failures on sale in kitchen shops.

Plate racks are potentially exciting examples of wooden engineering and can be tremendously rich visually because of the element of repetition, the shadows between the parts, the minutiae of the different pieces and the compacting of storage into a confined area. The china and crockery stored in them are often great to look at and use. So the racks are becoming increasingly popular and are part of the move away from the boxed-in, 'over-cupboarded' kitchen.

Teak is the wood used (with a suitable natural oil finish) where the plates sit especially on the horizontal elements. All constituent parts are designed for water to run off at angles, especially the horizontal ones such as the front and back bars in which the slots are made. I have also used teak on the sloping trays in which the cups and bowls sit with suitable run-off grooves. In other kitchens, expanded stainless steel sheet has proved useful because draining water passes between the rim of the cups and the surface.

The other parts can be any hard wood or metal where appropriate. To have easy-access, open storage seems better than stacking all the china in

This curved plate rack is an excellent means of providing accessible high-level storage, reflecting the circular base cabinet at eye-level.

This cupboard was wedge-shaped to respond to access between the two parts of the kitchen, and partly adapted to being a work surface. The granite runs right across.

cupboards, especially if it is in everyday use. Piles of plates need room above them so large amounts of space can be wasted, and they can easily get chipped.

The problem with plate racks is the multiplicity of different sizes and thicknesses of plates. It is impossible to find one design that fits all plates. The design may be adjustable to some extent or you may have to find plates to suit. Either way, the racks are worth making an effort to use.

CUPBOARDS AND DRESSERS

The term 'cupboard' is really a misnomer, certainly an accident of history. In the Middle Ages it described a series of 'bordes' for standing cups upon. Doors were presumably added later for security. 'Cupboards' at that time were known as aumbries, but this word had died out by the middle of the sixteenth century — subsumed by cupboard. In kitchens a variety of cupboard types are useful and mixing types is wise. I have developed several from historical prototypes and adapted them for kitchen use.

My modern adaptation of the court cupboard bears only some resemblance to its early predecessor conceived around the time of Elizabeth I. The name seems to have been derived, according to Ralph Edward Short's *Dictionary of English Furniture*, from the French *court* and its epithet 'short'. The main characteristic I have copied is that the court cupboard was designed in two or three tiers. In a kitchen a place to perch rather than formally sit down is often a great bonus. Visitors passing through like to chat and want to lean, perch or adopt a similar temporary posture, so I adapted the design to a three-tier cupboard with an extended lower front 'bench' which is used for storage as well. It is not too deep to prevent access to storage in the middle section of the cupboard. The top tier is the real cup 'borde'. By standing on the 'bench', the top tier is within easy reach for placing large, heavy items and so can be used for display or storage.

One reason I like the term court cupboard is that the royal connection implies a connection to those handsome, imposing cupboards that the early medieval castles must have had and that association is rather exalting. Although the term has fallen into disuse other than in the antique trade, I suspect that this is the reason that the term court cupboard gained popularity and was adopted as an epithet for short in the first place.

The parlour cupboard's historical antecedents are not quite so distinct, they were considered as two-tier or hall cupboards for use in living rooms, halls and parlours and were designed for storage of crockery and plates. In the process of designing a kitchen the last item is the inclusion of the table, often in cramped circumstances with little room left for a cupboard.

Nearly always storage nearby is needed for such items as table linen, mats, breakfast material and perhaps surplus or 'grand' china. Most people these days prefer to have their 'morning' china near the dishwasher so that putting away time is minimized.

My own version of the parlour cupboard is shallow and wall-mounted, allowing the cupboard to be tucked in behind the kitchen table where a standard-depth cupboard would be too big. As it is wall-mounted, a chair can be pulled back (the main cupboard part starts about the height of the average chair back) without the cupboard restricting the space between the table and wall. The supporting sub-structure with its turned poles and the 'roof' on the top recall the distinctive features of its antecedents with their bulbous turned cup and cover supports (shared with the court cupboard), heavy panelling, and wide mouldings particularly at the top. Wall-mounted cupboards have the advantage that they are economical with floor space – technically they don't use any but they do still effectively take up space.

Corner cupboards have long been a favourite of mine and are now becoming popular again. They have a necessary role. For a start they address the centre of the room and so can happily be adapted to house an appliance such as a refrigerator or oven, but they also work in sympathy

The parlour cupboard, shallow in depth and wall-mounted, can be used where space is at a premium, particularly behind a kitchen table. This was designed for Smallbone's unfitted kitchen.

The giant court cupboard conceals a refrigerator behind one inlaid, panelled door. The 'bench' area above the deep storage drawers forms a useful perch.

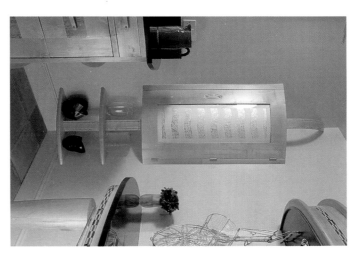

with the architecture of the room by making a feature of the corner. The corners of a room define the space and at least two should be left exposed or uncluttered if possible so that the architectural envelope remains distinct. If all the corners are used up, a very good compromise is to go for a wall-mounted or half-height corner cupboard where the floor and ceiling are left visible. They can make ideal drinks cabinets or spice cupboards with open shelves above their worktops.

Cupboards make a big impact on a space because of their large surfaces so they determine the ambience of the kitchen to a considerable extent. They are an opportunity to do something exciting. The choice of timber, or if painted the colour, is crucial. So too is the detailing, both inside and out. Inside adjustable shelves are sensible; these have to be made from veneered board construction (unless they are narrow) or they will warp. Putting a small raised 'tube' of solid wood on the front edge helps to prevent the odd spice jar from rolling on to the floor and also protects the edge of the shelf. Pull-out trays are an excellent way to improve access, especially in deep cupboards and are particularly useful if you have a large quantity of crockery, condiment or glass containers.

There are plenty of adaptations possible to make cupboards more useful and visually more interesting. Suspending a mini-table from the side to act as a breakfast bar; adding a brushing slide (a pull-out platform); putting in willow basket drawers; having part of the cupboard open (like in the seventeenth-century hall cupboards), perhaps with an open grille as in traditional food cupboards; mixing materials, using acid-etched glass in some panels and having an oversized cornice ... the list is long and exhaustive. Cupboards provide architectural punctuation and useful stor-

Corner cupboards such as this are a handsome way of using a corner but leaving the junctions with the floor and ceiling visible. The corners of a room define the architectural envelope (of a room).

RIGHT
The tallboy — my own version, using this ancient name for a tall piece of furniture, with willow baskets and an open dowelled top door panel, was designed for Smallbone's unfitted kitchen and has been widely copied. Even the lower plinth is a drawer.

FAR RIGHT
This detail shows carousels and a corner cupboard with wide grooves in the back of the door to prevent warping.

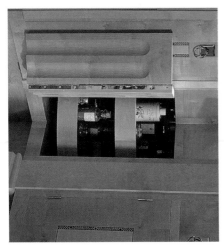

This recent design for a dresser at the entrance of a kitchen has hand-forged metal hooks and braces (see section entitled The Extended Kitchen).

BELOW
This design for a large painted dresser contrasts paint surfaces with wooden details in English olive ash. It was designed for Smallbone's unfitted kitchen.

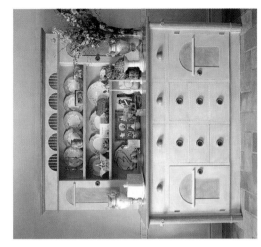

age – long live their development. Try, however, not to collect too many – you may end up without too much space to move about the room! New roads attract additional traffic, similarly cupboards with spare capacity soon get filled up.

Dressers are in my opinion one of the most adaptable, friendly and useful pieces of household furniture. The term derives from the French verb *dressoir*, to dress or prepare. Its first use dates from the 1550s when it was used to describe a sideboard or table in a kitchen on which food was dressed, surrounded by rows of shelves on which plates, dishes and so on were arranged. Ideally every kitchen should have a dresser because it adapts to so many needs from displaying Grandma's china to a jug holding pens and scissors, not to mention bowls of seasonal fruit and evidence of other culinary delights. A kitchen must have abundant visible evidence of its origins, and the dresser is one place where that can be done. A kitchen without a decent dresser – like all those fitted, standardized, plastic-laminated ones produced by the big industrial companies in the last few decades – are sad unhomely places.

CHOPPING BLOCKS & WASTE CHUTES

Every kitchen needs an end-grain chopping block. It is the only surface that will stand up to constant heavy-duty use for food preparation. When a knife is used to cut on an end-grain block, the impact is different from ordinary flat grain. The end-grain tends to grip the knife, rather than slide to one side, so it is safer to use. Flat grain on the other hand, tends to blunt the knife more quickly, causes more damage and deeper cut marks, so end-grain has a clear advantage.

Free-standing chopping blocks — as opposed to those built into central counters — are excellent, but you have to be tidy and well-organized. I have had the challenge of designing several free-standing chopping blocks that have multiple functions which in a small kitchen are useful — features such as pull-out trays underneath, pull-out worktops to the side, trolley wheels and built-in cupboards, drainers and waste bins. The most popular feature though has been the waste slot with the stainless steel container inserted in the drawer below so that it can easily be emptied. It enables you to get rid of scraps of waste food as you go, frees the work surface and provides a sense of order. It is also very convenient for breadcrumbs and so on that accumulate at breakfast and tea and saves getting out the dustpan and brush each time you clear up. The remnants can simply be swept into the slot.

Recently I have modified the design by using a pull-out drawer to the side (when possible) that can be opened when required so you can peel fruit and vegetables directly into the stainless steel insert without having to stand back from the worktop. This method avoids the need for a slot that causes interruption on the worktop.

In my first chopping block design the slot was too wide. It was made using end-grain block for a country kitchen in Gloucestershire.

This chopping block design (1980) using galvanized steel drawer and narrow waste slot, was designed with the encouragement of the Design Council to a low price for large-scale manufacture.

Central islands are preferable where possible to individual chopping blocks because other kitchen activities can be placed directly next to a chopping surface, but free-standing chopping blocks, carefully thought out, make an excellent second choice.

This chopping block was designed with an upstand to sit in the recess made by a tall panelled window (see section entitled Turning Obstacles into Opportunities).

The trapping of space between thin repetitive structural elements, like a bridge, makes for a dramatic centrepiece in a kitchen and also acts as a gantry for lighting equipment.

HANGING RACKS

These are among my favourite pieces of furniture because they can be almost sculptural being viewed from all sides, or at least three sides if they are wall-mounted. The hanging racks I design are open structures dedicated to good looks as well as function. The trapping of space within a network of thin elegant structural elements can produce exciting design that can enhance a central island and connect it to the architecture of the room, like a canopy does over a stove or a fireplace.

Their main function is a gantry for lighting. You need to have light in front of your eyes to prevent you working in shadow — especially on a working central counter. It is useful too for extra storage for small utensils — especially as so many are beautiful to look at. Why not hang them in a ready-to-use position? They also provide an opportunity to personalize

ABOVE

An arched hanging rack designed for the unfitted kitchen provides plenty of hanging space and in this case some shelves too.

BELOW

This rack is suspended over a sink cabinet with canework woven into the arch. Lighting equipment at the time was bulky and awkward to incorporate. Low voltage lighting has miniaturized the equipment.

ABOVE

An overhead canopy for an extractor combined with outriggers softens its impact in my own kitchen.

your kitchen either with your home-grown dried herbs or merely for all those minor objects that hang up and look nice, from dangling children's home-made objects to dried foods like garlic and onions.

Sometimes we build extractor systems into the gantries and an interesting balance is obtained between the enclosed box and its outriggers where the hanging element extends over the counter areas. The materials used vary from stainless steel, painted steel, hand-forged black steel to varying types of wood and painted finishes – all are chosen to blend in with the design.

ABOVE

The oval scoop handle — a
handle should invite you to use
it, catch the eye and be friendly
to touch.

RIGHT

The suitcase handle — this is
made in cherry wood with
specially designed stainless steel
spacers.

FAR RIGHT

The cleat handle — this is made
in stainless steel and inspired by
brat cleats. It is easy to grip top
or bottom and suitable for large
or heavy doors and drawers.

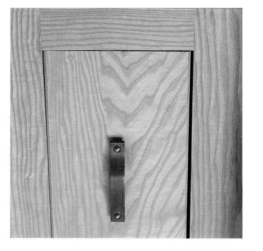

HANDLES

Handles provide a great opportunity to enhance a piece of furniture. They focus the eye, draw attention to a specific area, add visual interest and change the tone of the piece. They are also a point of contact for the hands, the tactile connection between the user and the piece of furniture. It is the part of the furniture you touch most often. You use them to reveal the inside, contents and all.

Variety is important. It is good to change the handles to fit in with their function, as well as aesthetically. A drawer requires a different handle to a door. The height and weight of the door also play a part when considering the design. A tall refrigerator needs a strong, big, easy-to-grasp handle. A small low-height cupboard door needs only a delicate handle. Drawers can take the finest handles which can be horizontal in shape, whereas an upright design is often best on vertical frames on doors.

The choice of material is important. Usually a contrast with the background material is desirable. Most essential though is that they should be a pleasure to use. They should feel comfortable, be easy to grip, preferably with at least four fingers, and be soft enough to enjoy holding, both in shape and material; it is obviously vital there should be nothing to catch clothes on or trap fingers inside. Ideally the design should be a pleasing piece of sculpture in its own right.

Hidden handles or secret grooves which became fashionable in the 1970s are, I feel, a sell-out and deprive the viewer or user of a certain level of enjoyment. Furniture without handles looks impoverished. 'Secret' drawers or doors are the exception and give an element of surprise to the design.

Handles can be extremely simple; just a small hole and a moulding cutter taken round the edge softens the edges and delights the eye.

BELOW

A turned knob is easy to grip and unselfconscious, and suitable for small cupboards. The profile needs to be thought out. There are many ugly versions on offer.

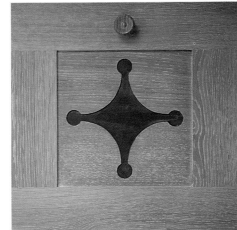

Circular-shaped sinks are made to suit whatever radius is needed. This one is made by Promart. The sinks are seamless, welded into the worktops.

WORKTOPS & SURFACES

A balance of different materials should make up kitchen work surfaces, each one chosen for its appropriateness first and then adjusted to the taste of the client and the aesthetic parameters of the design by choice of colour or type.

For the cooking area, granite or stainless steel is best; a few types of non-porous slate with a high quartz content are also useable.

For the wet areas around the sink, non-porous materials are best, but an alternative is a wood, such as teak from sustainably managed forests, which has a natural oil content that repels water. Well looked after and given the occasional coat of Danish oil, it provides the most pleasing surface to put dishes, glass and china on after washing them, especially if they are delicate (and so not suitable for the dishwasher). Some people who have granite tops around the sink place a tea-towel on them to 'soften' the surface.

If you use wooden tops, the sink must be mounted underneath the boards and the whole area should be detailed carefully so that the boards

This is a detail of the modern kitchen illustrated on page 148.

slope with grooves for draining the water into the bowl, making sure that there are no traps where the water can collect. In the area immediately around the taps we use a built-in granite tray so that should the taps leak or cause excessive wear to the 'oil' finish, surface damage is avoided.

For food preparation, end-grain hardwood, usually maple which is hard and even-grained, makes excellent chopping blocks. When wood is turned on its end, it provides a harder surface more resilient to cutting – almost to the point of not showing knife cuts at all. Butchers have been using such blocks for many a year – and in domestic premises they will last for ages.

Over the last decade or so I have come under attack for using wooden worktops on the grounds they are unhygienic. I have even been on the radio in the past to defend their use. I explained that at home my mother's kitchen (along with so many others of my and previous generations) had only wooden worktops and no member of my family ever had food poisoning because of them. Quite recently, I was thrilled to find my views justified in an article published in *New Scientist*. Two researchers at the University of Wisconsin conducted experiments subjecting work surfaces

The Belfast sink with a teak draining board – these need to be carefully detailed or the water will rot the wood. All surface water should naturally drain into the sink.

BELOW

End-grain hardwood, especially hornbeam, beech or maple, provides the most hard-wearing and hygienic preparation surfaces.

made of nine different species of wood and four sorts of plastic to bacteria such as salmonella, listeria and escherichia coli, initially for three minutes. The level of bacteria actually diminished on the timber while it remained unchanged on the plastic. After a whole night the bacteria on the wooden surfaces cleaned themselves thoroughly, but on the plastic they multiplied. To Dr Cliver and Ms Ak, the researchers, we owe a big debt. Wooden worktops are declared not only safe, but more effective in killing bacteria. Trees have spent millions of years fighting bacteria, and when a tree is cut down, its timber still remains 'alive' with its inherent anti-microbial organisms. Why didn't our common sense prevail earlier? Bureaucracy and science can make a lethal combination. From this information I would suggest natural oil finishes that breathe, or simply scrubbed wooden surfaces are more appropriate on worktops than heavy lacquers. Where wooden worktops are used as a servery or for display, such as shelves or fronts of cupboards, then lacquer still makes for a more polished finish.

Marble is a wonderful material and fine for pastry-making but reacts to food acids, alcohol and sugar, so is best kept away from intensively used areas. Tiled worktops are to be totally avoided and really are unhygienic! Tiles easily become unseated and the grouting is soft, deteriorates quickly and is hard to clean. I tend to avoid laminated plastic products which seem overpriced, ersatz and often not as durable as the natural alternative. Such surfaces also reflect light poorly and lack the subtle variation that comes with 'natural' materials. Occasionally we use Colourcore which is a solid plastic material for the floors of cupboard below a sink where wet buckets can cause water damage to wooden surfaces.

ACKNOWLEDGEMENTS

Special photography Peter Aprahamian and James Mortimer.

The Publisher would like to thank the following photographers, libraries and archives for their kind permission to reproduce the photographs in this book:

The Advertising Archives 45 right, 47 top, bottom left and bottom right.

Arcaid/Richard Bryant 32, 36, 37, 43, 45 bottom.

The Bridgeman Art Library/Ackerman and Johnson Ltd. London 25/Cheltenham Art Gallery and Museums, Glos. 20/Christie's, London 23, 28, 42/Giraudon/Musée des Beaux-Arts, Lille 15/Giraudon/Musée des Beaux-Arts, Rouen 41/Giraudon/Musée Reattu, Arles, France 27/Giraudon/Strasbourg Cathedral 25 right/Gavin Graham Gallery, London 35/Johnny van Haeften Gallery, London 22, 24/Josef Mensing Gallery, Hamm Rhynern 34/Museum of Fine Arts, Budapest 21/Private Collection 25 left, 29 bottom, 38 bottom/Stapleton Collection 29 top, 44/Victoria and Albert Museum, London 38 top/Wolverhampton Art Gallery, Staffs. 39.

Rupert Cavendish, London 168.

Johnny Grey 182, 183, all plans/Tim Beddow 200/Michel Focard de Fontefigueres 74, 75 right and bottom, 76 left, 76-77, 78, 79, 194, 167/Rosie Hayter 169 bottom/Will Hill 130, 131 top and bottom, 134, 134 left of centre and right of centre/Richard Holt 50-51, 124, 126, 127, 148 top, 150-151 bottom, 189 left, 196 top, 202 centre, 204/Katerina Kalogeraki 164, 166, 167 top, 168 right, 169/James Mortimer 13, 18, 52, 54, 55, 56-57, 58, 60, 61/Michael Nicholson 144, 145 bottom, 146, 147/Smallbone 105, 106-107, 108, 109, 110 left, centre and right, 111 top and bottom, 112, 113, 114, 115, 195 left and top right, 196, 197, 198, 200, 201 top right and right of centre/Richard Trevor 7, 80 left, 81, 82, 83, 84, 86 top left and bottom, 86-87, 87 top right, 88-89, 188 bottom right.

Robert Harding Picture Library/Simon Brown/Country Homes and Interiors 132.

National Trust Photographic Library 49/John Bethell 14, 48/Geoffrey Frosh 10-11/Andy Tryner 14/Mike Williams 31.

Trevor Richards 170, 171 top left and top right.

Bibliography

Catherine Beecher, *A Treatise on Domestic Economy* (Harper, New York, 1849)

Mary Douglas and Baron Ishewood, *World of Goods, Towards an Anthropology of Consumption* (Allen Lane, London 1978)

Paul Feyerabend, *Against Method* (Verso, London, 1979)

Christine Frederick, *New Housekeeping, Efficiency Studies in Home Management* (Doubleday, Page, Garden City, New York, 1914)

Lillian Gilbreth, *The Homemaker and Her Job* (USA, c.1850)

Katherine Girier, *Culture and Comfort, People, Parlors and Upholstery* (University of Massachusetts, USA, 1988)

James Gleick, *Chaos* (Abacus, London 1988)

Johnny Grey, *The Hardworking House* (Cassell, London, 1997)

Johnny Grey, *Home Design Workbooks: Kitchen* (Dorling Kindersley Limited, London 1997)

Robert Harbison, *Eccentric Spaces* (André Deutsch, London, 1977)

Osbert Lancaster, *Here of All Places* (John Murray, London, 1959)

John Lukac, *The Bourgeois Interior*; American Scholar, Vol. 39, No. 4

Mario Praz, *An Illustrated History of Interior Decoration, from Pompeii to Art Nouveau* (Thames & Hudson, New York, 1982)

Bernard Rudovsky, *Architects without Architecture* (Academy Edition, London, 1964)

Witold Rybczznski, *Home* (Viking Penguin, New York, 1987)

Fritz Schumacher, *Small is Beautiful* (Abacus, London 1975)

Ralph Edward Short, *Dictionary of English Furniture* (Country Life, Hamlyn, London, 1974)

G. M. Trevelyan, *An Illustrated English Social History*, Vol. 4 (Pelican, London, 1952)

Angus Wilkie, *Biedermeier* (Chatto and Windus, London, 1987)

Paul Zumthov, *Daily Life in Rembrandt's Holland*, translated by Simon Watson Taylor (Macmillan, New York, 1963)

Index